Praise for *The Man Who Whistled, The Woman Who Wished*

An exquisite piece of remembrance, brimming with life, and true to life. The lines dance. I've read some sections aloud for sheer pleasure. There is such joy here, and exuberance, dry wit, intimacy, roundness, whimsy, and generosity too, that you want to just keep reading these songs and sagas. A sparkling gem in an unpretentious setting.

> — from the Foreword by **Hal Calbom,** film producer, writer, and editor of Columbia River Reader Press

In *The Man Who Whistled, The Woman Who Wished,* Florence Sage regales us with stories from another era—days of wringer washing machines, wicker baby buggies, clawfoot tubs, and penny candy. She invites us into her Polish-Canadian family with poems both lighthearted ("Scrappy Pappy") and serious ("Screech & Scream"). Pull up a chair, pour a glass of vodka, and toast *na zdrowie* to this delightful collection.

> — **Margaret Chula**, winner of Haiku Society of America's National Book Award for *Grinding My Ink;* laureate author of *One Last Scherzo;* 14 additional books including *Firefly Lanterns: Twelve Years in Kyoto*

I read this poem cycle with all the delight one takes in the March, Ingalls, or Durrell families. These economical tales carry as much grit, reality, and pure fun in their lines as any of those family sagas manage in their hundreds of pages. There is pathos—aunties losing their loves to WWII, a Canadian father seeing his daughter off to America—but also whimsy, a fine eye for detail, and buckets of love all around. Best of all is the sheer grace of the writer's words.

> — **Robert Michael Pyle**, Guggenheim Fellow, Burroughs Medalist, 24 books of poems and prose, including *Wintergreen, Chinook & Chanterelle, Magdalena Mountain, The Tidewater Reach*

The Man Who Whistled,
The Woman Who Wished

A Polish-Canadian Story

Florence Sage

with
HIPFiSH Publications
Astoria, Oregon

This is a work of memory and imagination.

The Man Who Whistled, The Woman Who Wished:
A Polish-Canadian Story

Florence Sage
All rights reserved by the author, 2021
ISBN: 978-1-7361048-0-4

Cover & Interior Design: Dinah Urell, HIPFiSH Publications
Author Photo: Bob Pyle
Publisher: Gray Area Press with HIPFiSH Publications
Astoria Oregon USA
2021

Set in Palatino 10.75 pt and Mongolian Baiti 22 pt

Dedicated to Dad and Mom
Victor and Florence

first generation in Canada
from Polish immigrant parents
Anna and Basil, Frances and John

and to my third-generation daughter Victoria Helen

These stories are set in Hamilton, Ontario, Canada,
from the time when Vic and Flo met in 1939
and are written by their second-generation daughter
who flourished for 21 years in their warmhearted home.

About the lilting house and happy
as the grass was green

– from "Fern Hill" by Dylan Thomas, 1937

My Thanks To

Robert Michael Pyle of Grays River WA for expert advice and warm encouragement; Thane Tienson of Portland OR for angelic contribution to pre-publication; Ric's Poetry Mic in Astoria OR where many of these poems had a generous early audience; Hamilton Poetry Centre, Hamilton ON for inviting this poet twice to read a few at their autumn mic.

Dziękuję

"Nothing good lasted in the world," Lezhev thought,
"that's why you needed poets to grab it as it went flying by."
from The Polish Officer, Alan Furst, 1995

Foreword

I am thrilled and honored to comment on Florence Sage's *The Man Who Whistled, The Woman Who Wished*, which is an utter delight. It's a great thing to have praise leap to mind unbidden.

This splendid book, its tone bright and right, brims with sweet life without being saccharine or sentimental. There is lots of wry wit — sober too, but not rueful — in all the right places. You want to keep reading, no easy feat for most memoirs or family history which can be pretty heavy going. In her hands, the family story is compelling—literally, lovingly, true to life.

Like the ubiquitous Polish pork, *pierogi* and *golumpki* these savory memories appear in well-wrapped packages as 62 poems, large and small, to comprise a memoir-in-verse.

As more of a student of poetry than a practitioner, I am struck by how the author gains both concision and acceleration using the musicality of narrative verse. It goes trippingly, it doesn't bog down. The lines dance, and line breaks give breath and breadth and emphasis. I read whole sections aloud, with great pleasure.

Sage paints soundscapes and mindscapes, too, with quick, sure strokes. The background and frame for the poems is her young life and times in Hamilton, Ontario, 1940s to 1960s. The world is at war in the early '40s, with the fates of both old and new countries intermingled. In her home, Polish transliterates into Canadian English, amidst wafts of "that gentle Slavic language," supper (not dinner) tables are laden with old-and new-country fare. The pork and the potatoes, the Babcia grandmother, the girl learning math from her father's cribbage board, all jump to life. Not entirely easy; there are perils for kids: measles, chicken pox, mumps, tuberculosis, and the horror of polio.

But these are balanced by a roundedness of stories, whimsy and generosity too.

I felt I knew Flo and Vic almost immediately, the "chatty mother" and dad "quick with quips," the Polish-Canadian couple brought to life instantly, vividly, in their daughter's fond recollections: the mother stitching matching outfits on her Singer machine, the father planting trees for cherries and spitting their pits with relish onto the road.

Besides being an exquisite piece of remembrance at a distance, it must give the author great satisfaction to have set this down, to have captured and preserved and highlighted these moments from her parents' lives. There is such joy in it, and exuberance! It makes me happy for her.

The Man Who Whistled, The Woman Who Wished: A Polish-Canadian Story rewards both a leisurely dipping into its 62 lyric poems, and a few hours to experience its magic entirely. Florence Sage has produced a sparkling gem in an unpretentious setting, the intimacies of her reminiscences buoyed and brightened by the lilt of these grateful songs and sagas. As one lover of words to another, I am happy to help bring this book to you.

– Hal Calbom, Seattle, May 2020
Hal Calbom is a film producer, song writer, editor of Columbia River Reader Press, with the monthly feature, "People + Place." www.crreader.com

Contents

Foreword	ix
Introduction	xiii
Scrappy Pappy	17
Here Comes Vic	21
Another One	23
Baby Buggy	25
Screech & Scream	29
Mother Tongue	33
Home Operation	35
Polio Finds Us	37
Kindergarten Class	39
Mom & Pop Store	41
Moya, Moya, Moya, Mine	43
Four Flats	45
Farm Stand	47
Basil & Anna & Frank & Annie	51
On Dad's Side	53
Sitting the Kids	56
Dark Outside	57
Cribbage Lessons	58
Bum to Bum	60
Perils Left, Right and Center	61
Stomach Ache	64
Helen's Practice	65
Dad's Office	69
Anything to Declare?	72
Musicals at the Palace	73
The Queen's Birthday	74
The Catch	75
Pyrotechnics	76
Pass the Salt	77
Pork on the Table	79
Gone Fishing	82
Polish Weddings	85
Fatherly Care	86
Herbs in the Yard	87

Green Paint	89
Fireplace Demolition	90
Mom's New Carpet	91
Death Benefits	93
Song of the Birds	95
The Laundry Hustle	97
Shat in Your Hat	99
Father and Mother Christmas	100
Man from Manitoba	103
Flying Feet	104
The Singer	106
Boy Meets Bay	111
Tax Night in Canada	113
Must have been Moonglow	114
Good Shot!	115
Winter Coats	116
Hallway at Twilight	119
Toilet in the Trunk	120
No Spitting	121
Don't Go!	122
To Have Girls	123
Hop In	125
The Winnipeg House	126
Night Road in Montana	128
You Deserve It	129
Pork, Not So Much	130
Call Me	134
For the Future	135

Introduction

My first-generation Polish-Canadian parents were the inspiration for these anecdotes and stories. As I reflected and wrote, I came to love the two of them even more and to appreciate fully the lucky life they gave me in the 21 years I lived with them.

Reminiscing about life in your own family to this extent puts you in another time and place until it's done, a place that sometimes seems more real than your daily life. I found my memories to be not just about my family, but about "us" together. It made me into someone who is both a figure in these stories and an observer with a current point of view.

In spring of 2018, I began to think of little moments that I "ought to write down," like my father spitting a cheekful of cherry pits onto the road at a stoplight from his farm truck. That memory became the first written poem, "No Spitting." I expected a few more scenes, but they kept rolling into my head for nearly two years, and then, with the last five in spring 2020, there were 62 poems – some expansive, some sketches.

As I'm an active poet, the scenes came to me as narrative poems rather than as prose. To me, the soundscapes of poems, the rhythms, the echoes, the shifts of meaning, the half-pauses at line breaks, heighten and contain the stories.

But it's the stories that matter. With a touch of poetic license for the telling, these are true events and vignettes and personalities as I recall them. "Scrappy Pappy" opens the collection as the establishing story of Mom and Dad, and though the memories came in whatever order they chose, the poems are then arranged pretty well chronologically. Together they make up a story of a family in their place and time, but not so unlike others.

I had a long way back to reach. These events happened from 1939 to late in the 1960s, centred in Hamilton, Ontario, Canada.

In the '40s when I was a child, bread trucks and milk trucks went through the streets to fill the orders we left in the boxes built into our houses (cream on top for Mom's coffee), the ice man came weekly to our doors, and the rag man, vegetable man and the scissors grinder still called from their horse-drawn wagons. Three steel mills provided hard work for immigrant men. By the time I left in the early '60s, Hamilton had a population of 258,000 and the blended Tiger-Cats football team in Ivor Wynne Stadium three Grey Cups.

But the first years of the 1900s is when the story really began, when my four grandparents made their way from Russian-occupied Poland to a new life in Canada in their mid-teens, my father's parents a married couple going to Winnipeg Manitoba, my mother's parents single, first meeting in Montreal, then going to the Eastern Townships of the province of Quebec. In the mid-1930s both families moved for work to Hamilton, then Canada's steel center, where my parents met in their twenties at the Polish Hall.

My father Victor was the spirited man who whistled with heart, skill and satisfaction. My mother Florence was the lively woman who quietly wished for a sense of belonging and tranquility, and a night out for cards with her busy husband. I was the girl who watched them, more than I knew, and eventually became the woman who wrote these glimpses down.

Florence Sage
Astoria Oregon USA
2020

Notes: Where appropriate, Canadian spellings have been used to suit the time and place of the stories. For our mothers, we said "Mum" like Brits, but wrote "Mom" like Americans. For the most part, with apologies to my first language, Polish accent marks have been omitted; I'd never get it right!

Vic and Flo, October 6, 1939, Hamilton

Scrappy Pappy

My father brought home a new red truck one afternoon.
Often surprised our mother one way or another
with something he'd bought without marital discussion.
He had a good relationship with his credit union.

The truck wasn't actually new or entirely red, some red,
some rust on the rounded fenders, a couple of dents.
It was better than new, it was new to him and suitable
for his rented orchards a few miles out after the day shift
on heavy machines. A bit weathered, set good and wide
for crates and bushel baskets. Just right for a man who farms

as on both doors, a cartoon hillbilly in tri-color lacquer
with the requisite shaggy white beard, overalls, corncob pipe
– no kidding – clicked his heels for deep rural joy
somewhere in America, anathema to our mother,
but Dad's eyes glinted behind his round wire-rim specs:
a fine bargain and a pretty good joke.

Underneath the old fellow each door declared, big and bold,
Scrappy Pappy, since it had been a junk man's truck,
which we'd now call recycling or reclamation or reuse,
but our mother called "What will the neighbours think?"
We kids could have rooted for either side, so we didn't.

...

Our chatty mother was a social creature in a social world.
She always wished for a rise in status from the truck farm
with the family cow and the Polish Mom & Pop grocery
in Black Lake – the asbestos town at Thetford Mines
in Quebec –and then the family's apartments in Hamilton
at Ruth & Barton above their Okuloski Dry Goods store,
the job at the Woolworth's downtown before she married.
Just a little lift up the ladder, a first-generation longing,
not to be helped.

A man who owned one aging blue suit he called good
for Christmas concerts, weddings, funerals and church,
our father had no thought of status. Had his own way
of making things good, hustled like a man with a dream

in his head, lined things up, got things done, worked
his way around his wife, with and without her knowing,
disordered her life repeatedly, shook her precious certainty,
aiming for the long run past where she was looking,
and closed his eyes and whistled like a violin.

...

Smack in the middle of our mother's tidy scene
at the corner of Grosvenor and Maple,
ever her personal trickster, our father
parked Scrappy Pappy out front at the curb,

reminding my mother again
that in spite of the peonies in the garden,
the row of ferns on the generous brick porch,
our canopy of maples, Grace church at hand
for the cleaned-up kids and Dad as a sidesman,
the Royal Conservatory of Music across from our door,
she with her law office job, kids with good grades
and pushing the mower over the lawn, raking leaves,
and all the neighbours up and down the street
Canadian polite,

no matter how hard she tried for dignity,
and our mother did earnestly try,
life does not mold neatly into place and it won't stay put.

Especially when there's this scrappy man she dearly loves,
whistling over the classifieds at the kitchen table,
pencil poised.

Vic with classifieds, Ridge Road kitchen,
c. 1974

Scrappy Pappy

and his Family

Flo and kids, Maple Ave. front stairs,
dressed up for Uncle Ted's wedding,
c. 1948

Okuloskis 1929 - 1939

With Family Cow: Friend, Ted, Flo, Helen, Sherbrooke, Quebec, 1929

Flo at 19, Sherbrooke, Quebec, 1929

Flo and Family Friend Walter, 1939

Frances, John and Ted on farm, 1930s

Here Comes Vic

Wiktor Skrĕkowicz caught sight of *Florentyna Okuloska*
one night before they were Dad and Mom
at the Polish Hall on Barton Street
in full traditional costume with her folkdance club.
Forget-me-not eyes caught his from the stage,
the only blue in the world.

Her sleeves were puffed, her dirndl skirt white,
and ribbons flew from her apron and vest as she spun,
fists on her hips, the band of flowers slipping on her brow.
The strap across the instep barely held on her shoes
as she stomped her foot in his direction, shaking the boards,
Baltic Maiden at Dance to heated rustic music.
He looked at her as if he'd never seen a woman dance
and she smiled at him as if it were true.

Never mind the other girls in the line,
most younger, some cuter, none more lovely to my father.
This is it, stop looking, Vic. It was the tall one at the end
and he never changed his mind.

He courted his sweetheart at the family house on Gage,
tires screaming to a stop in what they called his hot rod,
and *Here comes Vic!* went up among the sisters.

Fresh, dark-haired and handsome, a good height for Flo,
and with a decent job at the mill in uncertain '39,
you'd say Vic was a catch
– and his eyes were almost indigo.

Her mother sat him down when he proposed marriage
to remind him one more time that her daughter
was older than he by nearly six years.
Said Vic, *I'm marrying Florence, not her age!*

The shower at the Polish Hall drew "a big and jovial crowd,"
it's reported by their nephew Jim, who was then all of four
and had a job bringing beer to the tables, but remembers
how an ebullient Flo, quite the dancer, "carried the night."

Their wedding portrait shows them proud and blushing
as if they'd just pulled off something terrific.

By three years on, they had a house and three kids,
their dance both domestic and whirling.
They took up hearts, cribbage, euchre and bridge,
most always playing partners
and learning the secrets in each other's blue eyes.

Another One

My mother didn't know she was having twins
until I emerged at Mount Hamilton Hospital
one morning in 1942: *Wait! Here comes another one!*
One heart always covered the other
under our doctor's stethoscope,
we lay that close, and the stethoscope
and the doctor's hands were all they had to go by.

The baby boy went first and backwards,
breech, the hard way, in there so tight,
thus learning vital determination at birth,
opening the way for me, the girl, to slide right out,
my first debt and deep apology to my brother.

Our parents were so stunned at twins, they named us
after themselves, adding complication to the house
and our identities. How would it be for my mother to hear
her own name in her own voice down an evening street?

This after first naming us Mary and John to get us out
of the hospital, Mary outweighing John by two ounces.

Mom's third child in a year – girl, boy, oops, me –
I was either her happy surprise package or the last straw,
depending on her punishing migraines – how she'd rush
away upstairs and hang her head over the bed –
Dad's 12-hour shifts, and someone there to listen.
Mom and I were unsure for quite awhile how to play it.

But as we twins learned good tricks
from our more advanced and experimental sister,
like how to tip a porridge bowl over your head
and everybody in the row of high chairs giggles,
and even better, vegetable soup with noodles,
there came to be more times when Mom just sighed,
You Kids! More often called all three names together:
Felicia Florence & Victor, and three heads turned.

And then the third ambivalent child was content
to belong to the bunch, always an arm
around her back from her brother or her sister.
So "another one" became a lucky girl instead

and our Mommy read stories to us
in a group huddle on the couch,
Maggie Muggins, Just Mary, The Little Tug,
until the Happy Gang came on the radio
every school day after lunch.

Baby Buggy

When our mother had her third child
not quite three years into her marriage,
both joyous and stunned,
our sister only 11 months old when Mom had us twins,
her Uncle Felix brought her a double baby buggy.

A stately carriage, 3x3 wicker basket lacquered navy blue,
on large spoke wheels, handle across to rock up and down
as you walk, a hood against rain and too much sun,
you could fit three babies in with room to grow
for an elegant ride, which our mother did.

...

She dressed us three in identical clothes she'd sewed,
bibbed pants and skirts, wool jackets and capes.
Stylish herself when young, sewing for herself,
she knew how to cut a figure.

Through the rose garden at Gage Park and the bowling green,
along Main to the Delta and back on King,
past Polish George's tiny news shop where later we'd run
down the gravel alley for a *gazeta* and a Mello Roll in a cone,
an eye on the little jars of candies with our extra pennies.
George would make us ask in Polish to get served, *prosze pan*.
Along Grace church filling the block between Maple and King
the buggy rolled, to Mr. Naylor's corner grocery store
where the bell rang over the door and Mom had an account.

Long proud outings they were, and everybody looked,
often stopped and remarked because we were a pretty scene,
and nothing could please our mother more.

After all, it was a lot of work, three babies at a time,
husband six days on long shifts at the steel mill,
you'd merit a little attention.

Countless cotton diapers with a wringer washer
she was glad to have, clothesline on a pulley with pegs,
socks and boots and snowsuits on and off times three,
sewing our matching outfits on the Singer,
getting us bathed in the claw-foot tub
and fed and pyjamaed and into clean beds,
the three-way birthday parties in the yard,
canning in the kitchen, making supper for Dad
and cleaning up, and everything else in the house,
and taking us out for visits,
and I'm sure I've left things out, how did she do it!

...

Her youngest sister went back to work, bringing our cousin
to Mom to watch before baby Michele could walk,
and my sister was displaced from the buggy.

She leans against the side in a photo from the time,
a little frown, maybe the sun, maybe an inner conversation,
feet steady and sturdy in Buster Browns,
her hair held in ribbons and mine still downy as a duckling's.
There stands my tall composed sister Felicia Ann,
just about ready—unsure but she'll do it —
to give her place up
to the three silly babies in the buggy and walk.

War Years

Okuloskis: Ted, Helen, Flo, Joanne, Frances, Victor; Gage Ave. backyard

Arms full of kids at Gage Ave. house

Three Heads Turn: working at fireplace in dining room

Baby Buggy: Felicia, Florence, cousin Michele, Victor

Vic and Flo, 1945

Vic with his kids and mother Anna, 1944

Celebrating birthdays, twins' 5th, Felicia's 6th, with cousin Michelle, Maple Ave. party lawn

Screech & Scream

Fighter planes rumbled over our heads in the early 1940s.
With Canada a commonwealth ally in the European war,
the RCAF was training the Allied pilots and crew
over southern Ontario, especially to navigate at night.

Whenever a plane roared over our house
from the nearby Mount Hope airfield,
the lumbering yellow training planes
the heavy Harvards, and the Lancaster Bombers,
grumbling four-engine night fliers built in nearby Malton,
I threw myself down to the ground in desolation
and screamed, my arms covering my head.

Screeched and screamed

my mother told everyone, always getting the most
out of the story, but she was probably right
about the drama.

...

With a wonky back, our father was "not required to report
for military training," said the letter from Toronto in 1944.
But almost-uncle Chester Rozak's two-seater training plane
went down in an Ontario farmer's field by Camp Borden
as he shouted instructions to his young trainee pilot
from the back seat; the plane dove and didn't pull up,
they were gone.

We kids lost our Godfather Chester, christening delayed
until our early teens, in time for Anglican confirmation
in the church across the street. Risking our souls,
the nervous tutted. No longer a baby to be spoken for,
though, I got to choose my own middle name at the font.

Auntie Helen lost the most. Chester was her best beau ever
and she never married. Already appearing in family photos,
he might have had a ring in his dresser.

Uncle Zbigniew Bar had joined the fight to fly
with the English RAF in the Polish Krakow division,
Poles hoping to shorten the war against their homeland.

He wooed my mother's youngest sister fair Joanne
at the Mount Hope airfield dances held for the trainees,
a striking match, the bride in flowers.

I picture a Polish aviator, slick dark hair and moustache,
lithe of body, and speaking soft consonants. Handsome,
those Poles in blue uniforms trimmed with gold
when they snapped to attention and clicked their heels
in courtesy at the front door, arriving full of conversation
in twos and threes for hospitable Polish family dinners.

The war too compelling to let go, he soon volunteered
to fly supplies to drop into the starving Warsaw ghetto.
He got shot down over Romania, his widow heard,
though she never was officially told; it was a secret.

Life went bad for his wife, suddenly a Polish widow,
and the tiny baby named Michele he'd left in Canada.
Joanne applied to recover her Canadian citizenship
and too soon remarried, cloaked in sadness.

I mean, was I wrong to scream?

Poles helping the Allied cause in several countries,
my mother's cousin Bronek served with the Polish army
in Italy to break Mussolini, and came straight to us
in Canada at the end of the war, never back
to his Russian-occupied homeland.

His wife Stella was kept for 15 years more
behind the Iron Curtain, drawn across in front of her
when Stalin was handed Poland after the war as Stella
looked west with all her heart where her husband was.

More and more money was demanded to get her out.
Our grandmother paid it; The Tsar, Stalin, Khrushchev
the apparatchik, she understood tyrants.

We welcomed Stella in Auntie Helen's rec room
in 1960 with an Okuloski feast, where Stella smiled
and nodded in the way of my father's shy mother Anna,
sitting pleased among us with her few English phrases,
unable to follow the language and the boisterous family.

I was 18. I sewed a new dress to meet her, textured white
with blue embroidered flowers, and even lapels.
She'd arrived middle-aged with just a suitcase.
There were toasts and presents like a bridal shower.

...

A reluctant screamer in the '40s, my nerves primed
by wartime planes, I extended my screams to Uncle Roy,
his bushy black moustache startling me, Mom said,
when he poked his head through the door and spoke to her
while she gave me a bath, and set me off in toddler panic.
Oh, it took me years to stop.

Then it was Rose and Roy's noble Newfie Boots,
luxurious long black coat, white chest and feet,
who knocked me over with her heavy fringed tail
just wagging to see us, wasn't she, lovely Boots.
I stood on Aunt Rose's kitchen table to scream,
though Roy, moustache, and I were reaching peace.

Head carpenter at Robinson's department store,
he built us girls a wooden dollhouse three feet tall,
just my size, with several rooms and tiny furniture,
for years after Sunday supper my world to arrange,
and Mom would carry up Sunday night banana cake.

I hoped it would soon be over, such a baby screaming.
Boots, who wouldn't harm a bird or any baby,
a contented giant in our midst
as the picture in *The Spectator* years later showed: Boots
on a blanket beside a robin, baby cousin Jan in a bonnet,
an idyll in the shaded garden
by Rose's goldfish pond on Emerald North.

...

Aside from the ashtray stand in our living room
made from the shell of an aerial bomb,
and lingering wartime expressions that my mother kept

   – So? Sew buttons for the Red Cross! –

the war fell behind us as if we'd forgotten.

I grew taller and embraced old Boots around her neck,
had my school, soft-shoe ballet, my stories and
my sister for secrets, muffled laughs and scraps
in the too-small-for-us double bed, my brother
to play tin soldiers and tanks, checkers and silly,
Mom making her chewy soups, her merry laugh,
all our Sunday outings with Dad at the wheel,
and most everything seemed to get funnier with time.

Mother Tongue

I'm told we spoke "pure Warsaw" Polish like our parents
before we spoke English as second-generation kids.
But before we turned four, our Polish stopped.
Experts in the '40s said one language at a time for success
and peace at school. *It's Canada, switch to English.*

Our concerned parents set aside the obvious fact
that they and their siblings were perfectly bilingual
with no accent either way, my father so exact in both
he was a translator for the court in his crisp Canadian
and immaculate Polish, and his very good ear.
They listened to the experts, as worried parents do.

As we took on a new language and school,
we left Polish behind. Our parents kept it
to themselves for private conversation.
To us they gave the rhythms, the scales,
the precision of Canadian English for life.

My brother became a Renaissance scholar.
Why do you not study Polish literature?
he was asked by a friend of our Aunt's.
Because we lived in English, the voice
of our bodies, our minds and souls,
our poetry and prose, we were Canadian.

Still, I carry a sense of something lovely lost
as you might in your dreams.

What I have left of that gentle Slavic language
are words a little child would know: several ways
to say goodbye and hello, come here, wait,
yes and no, good morning, good night, good God,
go to sleep, you children, daughters and sons;
eggs, potatoes, milk, and always tea
on the evening table in our house, and bread and toast;
Grandma, a most important word for any child,
my blanket, my doll, my daddy and mommy

and even how are you, Mr. and Mrs.?
Baby Polish: What else does a little girl need?

I can't get titles, names and noun endings right
—not even my mother's—the genders and cases,
or conjugate verbs, past, present, future,
or read all 32 letters or use the 17 diacritic signs,
as we kids never got as far as reading in Polish.

I can't hold an adult conversation. Proven
on a train from Warsaw to Krakow in 2007
on my nostalgic first visit to look around.
We went to English embarrassingly soon. I lacked
the Polish words and grammar. I was crushed.
Slavic is complicated. I consider my ancestors geniuses.

But in deference to our past, I always attempt to say
a written word by ear and how it feels in the mouth
—my mouth with its own better memory—
making my slow way through a train of consonants,
and my tongue can still flutter the Polish R off the front,
like the first note of a satisfied cat.

Surprised by a tourist family speaking Polish
in my town out on the coast
I hear those soft consonants catch my ear
and I stop to listen
and my chest swells
and my eyes well up
and I say hello
and long to tell them my grandparents' story
—in Polish, our mother tongue.

Home Operation

G. G. Henry, MD, the G's for Gladstone and Goldwin,
arrived one afternoon at our house with his big medical bag,
winter of '46, days into a record Hamilton snowstorm.

Family doctor to all our relatives, liberal with his house calls,
he would do an incision on my brother and me at home.
Hospitals full of troops. We'd be on our own beds.

Dr. Henry slogged through to King George School,
a military hospital at the end of WWII where soldiers
lay in rows on their way home from defending
Western Europe—my grandparents' homeland Poland
deemed too far, too foreign and hopeless to help.

Dr. Henry talked the military docs into giving him
what he said was one of the first tubes of penicillin ointment
released to citizens in Canada.

A cautious and dignified man, he'd pleaded his case:
Two kids with a dangerous infection,
abscesses sulfa hadn't touched,
he cared for us and ours, please, a little help.

Wet past his knees, galoshes full, snow swirling and deep,
car left back on Main, he walked the new drug
down our snowed-in street to us.

Dad got the day off work at the mill. He had one assignment
while Mom circulated with gauze and towels and water
and soothing hands and words for everyone
that afternoon and for ensuing weeks, ongoing
bandages and the ointment for her two little patients.

Dad, through each procedure, was to hold our feet,
first my brother's, then mine, while Dr. Henry worked.
Might have been as Dr. Henry said, to keep us still, but
just as likely to give our father something useful to do.
Not easy to watch your four-year-old twins through this.

I swam up from the dark world of ether to see my father
frowning down, doing his job, gripping hard,
still afraid to look away from my feet.

Daddy, I'm awake now, I piped, sitting up
and reaching to unclench his machinist's hands
from my ankles and shift his focus.
My father at my feet, his distress on his face,
young as I was, I knew right then
we'd understand each other better.

I carry the scars by my ear from a reasonable sew-up
in sub-optimal conditions,
distinguishing marks and memories, not to erase,
in case I should ever forget or lose myself or my father.
And not such a bad story either, the kind you keep
in case anyone asks.

Polio Finds Us

Before the Salk vaccine changed the world
my sister was struck with polio.

Not the polio that leaves you crippled
with steel leg braces, or alone in an Iron Lung,
but the kind in your brainstem that spikes your fever
and it comes down in time and you're alright,
you can wake up, you can breathe, you can walk,
or it doesn't and you're gone.

Polio was the viral wolf waiting for kids
at the pool, the church, the school, the store
and polio came through our door.

Stepping out of the Delta Theatre movie matinee
my sister Felicia frowned against the sun:
I've got a really bad headache, Mom.

...

Our parents were forced to give her up
to Hamilton General Hospital for several weeks,
a sick little girl, her family at home
and little explanation, though she remembered
the nurses were kind and jolly as they checked her legs.

Mom and Dad were only allowed to wave at her
from the sidewalk underneath her window
several floors up, and she would wave back down,
but only at visiting hours. That's all they got.
The hospital was saviour and also the boss.

Passing the crisis but not out of danger
she made herself at home, livened the place up,
and over the weeks got wiser than her years.
She made friends with the granddads on the wards
who adored her solemn demeanor and frown,
the kick of a smart little girl hopping among them.

The rest of the family were quarantined at home,
a rare and drastic measure at the time,
except that our father was allowed to drive to work,
no family sick leave or compensation.

Our sibling birthday party that summer was spread
out under the maples on the side lawn
while we household remnant presided on the verandah,
our cousins and aunts and uncles waving up at us,
missing our companion sister, but nothing to do
but wait.
...

We cheered in my classroom in grade eight,
and some teachers shed tears,
when the principal announced over the PA
that Salk had made a polio vaccine.

At 18 my sister trained as a nurse, familiar territory
on the wards, back to cheering up the old folks.
With the *dziadeks*, she used the expressions
we'd often heard from Dad, unaware they were jokes,
rough Polish-English puns. "How are you doing?"
came out in his Polish as "How's the man blowing?"
but much less polite.

Eyebrows lifted: *what a bold young nurse,*
until one astonished patient told her
that Dad must have been playing with words.
We quit using Dad's hybrid Polish.

Polio left me wary of summer matinees
but my sister likes to say she *turned the page.*

Kindergarten Class

So he stood in his shoes/And he wonder'd /He wonder'd /He stood in his/ Shoes and he wonder'd – **John Keats, "A Song About Myself," in a letter to young Victor from Miss Bryant, our second-grade teacher**

The boys are running in a fevered circle
in the big room along the back of the school,
leather shoes thumping on the polished wood floor,
voices ringing high against the green plaster walls,
little boys in kindergarten in corduroy and wool, just five
and full of little boys' thoughts and jumping beans.
The teachers hope the game will calm them down.

My brother reaches forward and swats the rump ahead
on the run, a variation on the game to his eager young mind
just extra fun, but the boy protests and Victor's been seen,
and a teacher swoops in to pull him out of the circle,
and the miscreant gets a talking to and a swat of his own,
an intentional spank, that one, not in fun. In those days
the principal kept a leather strap in his office for your hands.

Kindly man, returned from the Great War
with a steel plate in his head,
he had no taste for the strap, but it was protocol
if you'd been bad enough.

...

I open my arms and he tumbles in, my brother twin,
tears in his eyes for being misunderstood, wondering boy
just trying something out, for the fun,
and we sit just so for a moment, just us, that's how it was.

You'd never know how we scrapped at home.

But one of the teachers says, *No! Don't comfort him!*
I give her a look to wither the plant on her desk,
as much as I can manage without trouble for myself,
a useful look I will later practice, risking
the image of teacher's favourite my mother and I enjoyed.

I, the peachy blondie girl sent down the block to school
in careful morning ringlets and milk-chocolate stockings,
a pleated skirt, earnest in my schooling, a follower of rules,
I was to stand in front of the whole class of 30 little kids,
raise my baton and wave the rhythm instruments in on time,
now sticks, now triangles, now tambourines, now drums,
keep the beat, doing fine,
unless I hadn't slept so well the night before,
which such responsibility can do – I was only five too—

and I would cross the stage in something pink made by Mom
to lead the band in the Christmas concert with pretty aplomb
and a curtsy—a little Canadian royalist.
Boys jostled at story time to sit beside
the girl I was, even though
she peed in her yellow clown suit on Halloween.

That favoured little girl, to her relief, had the class credibility
to defy injustice the way her father would have done
and all the Polish fighters in the stories,
her arm firm around her wronged brother, his face buried.

No one was sent to the office,
and no one reported any of it to Mom,
who would have been torn in her duty, like any mother,
to raise nice acceptable kids, good little Cubs and Brownies,
and at the same time understand in her heart
who we were and what we did that day
that the teachers didn't like.

Mom & Pop Store

Our *Babcia* Okuloski, we said it like *Bahp'-cha*,
had her womanly grit and steel from early on,
coming over from Poland before 1905, just 16
and on her own, to join her sister Rose in Montreal,
routed through the foreign challenges of Ellis Island.
In her first job as maid to "a high New York Polish family"
she served dinner to renowned violinist Ignacy Paderewski.
When she got to Montreal she was introduced to John
and got down to what she'd really come for.

New Canadians, the couple raised five Canadian kids,
bilingual from the streets, my mother the first, born in 1910,
and opened a series of three grocery and dry-goods stores
as they moved from town to town to industrial city.
Frances oversaw, helping out her husband, who drank
but had an eye for good stock and customer fairness.

They recruited their eldest, my mother, to care for the house
and her four younger siblings when not in school.
The times called for practicality and considerable sternness.

...

A formal portrait by the first store in Black Lake Quebec,
marked 1912, shows two sober sculpted faces, maybe proud,
the "Mom and Pop" posed together on the wooden sidewalk,
staring light-eyed at the slow shutter, their erect posture
fixed for posterity.

Proprietor husband in high collar, white shirt, a vest and tie,
his white apron draped from waist to ankles.
At his shoulders two metal posters on the clapboard say
Smoke Rose Quesnel Tobacco, another announces Polo Plug,
and the fourth is for Labour King tobacco chew,
a big plug or twist 5¢.

A successful store for the mining families
from the Thetford asbestos mine nearby.

In the '50s we'd find a keepsake rock marbled with asbestos
deep in Grandma's dresser drawer in Hamilton on Gage.

Posing three steps to the left of John, hair piled up, Frances
in her mutton-sleeved lace wedding dress dyed green
for further use. We keep it in my mother's cedar chest.

Between them, standing on a chair, a flaxen two-year-old
dangling a cat from one arm, possibly perplexed
by the camera apparatus and the man disappearing
under the black cloth with the command to hold still,
unaware as yet of all the effort and joy ahead,
my little mother.

Moja Moja Moja, Mine

In grandmother years, an unguarded woman emerged
for us kids: warmth, embraces, time-softened eyes,
enigmatic little shrug and smile, white braided crown,
flowered wool kerchief, cotton stockings, black coat,
the very picture of a *Babcia*, a little lost in our era.
One at a time she'd gather us kids in to rock
in her arms, *moja malenka, moja moja moja, moj.*

My cousin Michele she called her raspberry,
moja Malina, and me in her arms she called *Lotsi.*
I took it for granted then
though it's not any version of my name: Florence,
Florentyna, or Florça for short at home; Florence
for school and neighborhood; Flo for Girl Guides.
A search says Lotsi is a pet name used in Ukraine.

Ukraina! Out came the steel behind the sweet.
My grandmother said nothing good about Ukrainians.
She once tried to persuade my teenage cousin Jim to drop
his pretty Ukrainian girlfriend for *a Canadian girl,*
which he did of his own accord at the right time
for his own reasons, for Mary.

Did it matter to Grandma that the bear of Russia clawed
up Poland and "all the Russias" as his reward for WWII,
her birth village Zbarosch given to Ukraine for the Soviet
in spite of all the Poles had done for the West in the war,
and what the Russians had done to the Poles?
Another murdering tyrant to the East to be placated,
as bad as the Tsar she'd left behind.

Did it really matter, after centuries of grabs and repression
back and forth: Cossacks, Mongols, Austrians, Hungarians,
Prussians, Romanians, Russians, Lithuanians,
and Poland even, once empiric itself, large and grand,
and at another time completely gone?
Where do you start over there?
Expect borders to be weak and a little tense.

The *Polska* in the soul that never changed
with the map was in my grandmother's birth,
The Ukraine right next door
and long claimed by the Eastern Slavs,
its very name Ukraine meaning *Borderlands*,
the countries have spilled each other's blood.
You can expect old Polish mistrust to linger
until the Soviet came apart after her time.

What of Lotsi, then? Let's say my *Babcia* simply
gave me that sweet name as a gift from the past.
The Ukrainians don't own the name,
and they have their troubles and hearthaches too,
so thank you, *dyakuyu duzhe*, I'll take it.

Four Flats

Just after the war, 1947 or '48, lots of goods on rationing:
meat, bread, sugar, lard and butter, forget your cakes,
tea, cheese, eggs and any what-have-you's,
and *Sorry no coffee*, and everything that came in cans,
so Canada could help feed the war-ravaged in Europe,
our hearts went out, and gas,
and 11 million households kept gardens and ration books.

Also tires and the rubber and the patches, but
you couldn't get those "for love nor money,"
nor tokens nor coupons, not as civilians.
To the good, it kept us families close to home, when
after that second world war, home sounded pretty good.

...

Nevertheless, we family of five took a road trip
to Trenton RCAF base to visit an old friend of Dad's,
Lee, an air force man, who had served in the war
when Dad couldn't. A base was a novelty to us.

Dad behind the wheel, as Mom never got a license.
First time she drove on the farm, she ran the Ford
into a field, which stopped the car. Gripping the wheel
with gales of laughter, she forgot how to brake.
She and Dad changed seats. Later on, when she tried
to practice, we three kids howled distress
beyond understanding, something deeply wrong
with Mommy driving, the Backseat Furies wailed.

Our father accepted his role as chauffeur and companion
on call when he would otherwise have been working.
Not driving could have been her most brilliant marital idea.

...

A wartime tire went *bang* on the long road to Trenton
and out came a second-hand patch, or maybe third.

Mom kept her young kids entertained in a field,
wisely having brought a picnic and some books.

Back on the road, *bang* again, repeat the fix,
another *bang* and then one more, *bang* the fourth,
the food and drinks having by then run out and Mom
losing her magic, songs and stories worn aerogram thin.

The long drive took twice as long as it should,
yielding for the family Brownie, more so with every stop,
a mother with a fixed grin, three smeared frowning kids
and a father on a tire pump gritting his teeth at the lens,
a trip to remember in the four black and whites
Mom would keep for us all in her picture box.

Farm Stand

In the Kodaks, the men pause with hands on their suspenders
and the older women sit in floral cottons, our mother
in T-shirt and slacks, everyone sweaty and squinting
in front of the shack, gathering spot with lunch and lemonade.

Years later, Dad showed me, the land became a subdivision,
the shack still standing as a curiosity. At the time of the snaps
it was the family's small strip farm to work on weekends
near the junction of Ontario Hwy 8 and 20.

Grandmother Frances with braided crown casts her eyes
at her husband John, maybe rye on his breath from his flask,
who nevertheless watched over the farm, working catalogues
to his dying day for the best fruit and vegetable plants
and he packed the berries tight – our grandfather standing
round and tall and proud for the photos.

Our genial Mom and Dad, Flo and Vic or Vic and Flo,
depending, a sister, Helen or Joanne. Mom's Uncle Felix
arrived in his 30s black Dodge coupe and summer fedora.
Her cousin from the Old Country, Bronek,
who'd made his way to us from the Polish army
serving with the Allies in Italy
and still hoped and waited for his wife.
Sometimes the grands from Dad's side, Basil who learned
enough English at the mill for a little conversation,
and Anna with her few useful phrases and good nature.

Born on farms all knew what to do. In kerchiefs or straw hats
they rolled up their sleeves and pants, to tan, tend and pick,
and everyone took baskets home.
It was our 5.5 acres of fertile common ground.

...

As baskets filled, Mom's sister Helen in her '40s shorts
and a wide brimmed straw hat, graceful and slim,
pulled her shirt off to reveal a black velvet bathing suit top,
the strap circling the back of the neck for a portrait
sort of décolletage,

called us kids down from the apples or across the creek,
bruised, scraped, and smudged with our youth and berries,
three sun-lightened blonds and one wavy brown like her,
girls with frizz escaping ribbons, boy streaked with dirt.

We trucked to the highway laden to stock the farm stand.
Of all the pretty fruit and veg, I was proudest
of the potatoes we dug, learning from Grandma
which were for selling and which were for seed.

A winsome tableau we made for cars on Highway 8,
the bait
the velvet top, the tan, the tousled assistants
orchard-messy in matching overalls,
a line of buyers developing on the shoulder.

Auntie Helen, who would make her millions at law,
diligent, methodical, detailed, QC correct,
she knew what to do, moved the goods
with clever words and kids
and bathing suit.

I acquired a lifelong taste for peaches and plums that run
down your face, tomatoes that smell like their stems,
greens over half my plate, potatoes any way they come,
and a disconcerting taste for being the bait.

Kids on the Farm

To Have Girls:
Vic with Felicia and Florence

Felicia, cousin Michele, Victor, Florence

String of Kids

Kids with cousin Jim on a Sunday outing

Basil & Anna & *Frank & Annie*

Maybe he called her *Annie* that day in March in Winnipeg
when they went to register their first son's birth in 1916,
feeling sweet, and maybe it amused her to call him *Frank*.
Or maybe the boss or the boys at the car repair shop
didn't like *Basil Skrěkowicz* so much,
so good-old *Frank* was my grandfather's self-defense
and he used it that day with the Anglo recorder,
maybe that's how it was.

Frank and *Annie* were what the official wrote,
names I never heard my grandparents called,
though to be honest, I didn't know
until a winter day in 2018 looking at old papers
that her last name had been Haidasz,
and neglected to ask,
though I knew Grandma Frances had been a Pisarski.
I came to Anna decades too late.

...

That's how my father's birth certificate came down,
possibly with wrong names for his parents, possibly not,
and the last name a bit misspelled, just a "t" for a "c,"
though in fairness, some *Skretkowicz* at some time
did adjust the middle to deal with the very foreign
accent mark that nobody knew how to use,

foreshadowing for Dad and the rest of us the spelling
variations in every news clip and report card ahead.
Usually, Dad's first name Victor was right, and his son's,
our girls' names too, and Mom's, in the paper and school,
with at least the "S" to start the surname,
so we'd know they meant us in the jumble that followed.

The spelling error recording my dad's birth
would be fixed at Wentworth county courthouse
in 1940 by his new sister-in-law Helen the lawyer,
but we all came to expect and accept the many

well-intended pronunciations and approximations.
You have to have the ear and experience and vision
for unaccustomed names, and really want to remember.

...

"Poland, Austria," was recorded as place of birth
for Dad's parents, and that was correct on the map,
as Poland was diminished when they were born,
Basil in 1890, Anna 1893, aka *Frank* and *Annie*.

But in a country eaten-at, sometimes devoured,
by empirical neighbours
Poles learned to carry and nurture
the *idea of Poland* as much as the land itself.

Though they'd left it as teens
their roots and hearts remained in *Polska*,
more Polish than Canadian to the end, those two,
so I knew too little about them.

On Dad's Side

Two of the sons of Anna and Basil, the Skretkowicz side,
gravitated like circling moons to the families of their wives.
Could Vic resist the robust Okuloskis, or Walter the Bonks?
The middle son Ben's wife had no family nearby;
they led a quiet life with their two in Stoney Creek.
We kids didn't see much of Dad's side of the family.

Not even our grandparents, who kept to themselves,
lonely in the Anglo end of the city a few blocks from us.
Once within the range of adolescence and memory and guilt,
we were perplexed how to talk to our *Babcia* Anna –
her high *heh, heh, heh, heh, heh,*
a few phrases of shy English and Polish to pass between us.
Sparse visits we made to her – in our neglectful teens.
We never even offered to walk with her to Loblaws.

Sometimes our mother convinced one of us to come along,
Anna nervous with her Canadian grandchildren
in the dark heavy room, crochet on the chair arms and backs.
Mom translated our grandma's thin nasal as Anna nodded,
agreeable behind her tiny wire glasses
and we drank black tea with milk and tried not to break
her porcelain cups and religious figurines.

...

But there were Christmas Eves when we were small.
Cousins conspired under the table on the straw put down
for the cattle in the stable. Granddad carried us on his back
as in Polish we called him *Horsie.* Our grandmother,
hair rolled sausage tight around the bottom of her head,
two steel safety pins holding an apron bib to her chest,
crushed us to her in the kitchen for the holiday

then set herself apart, never sat, countenanced no help,
and brought out labour-intensive dishes, per tradition:
pierogi with several fillings: potatoes with cheese, cabbage,
cherries, even swoony prunes – and meaty rice *golumpki,*
all with buttery onions and sour cream.

Easter dinner, which the Okuloski family ignored,
freeing our parents to visit Dad's side, began
at the elder Skretkowicz house with hard-boiled eggs,
as required, and wafer-thin bread as if we were at Mass
and then roast lamb for the Lamb of God.

Lapsed as a Catholic, our practical father
had gone Anglican with us right across Maple Ave.
Mom's parents were Church of Poland,
so why should we not be Church of England at Grace,
the church so handy, Canon Ferris walked past our house,
and in the annex, Brownies, Cubs, Girl Guides, Scouts.
Really, the lamb worked all around.

...

On those holidays Basil coaxed our mother to take
a stiff drink for the standing toast before the meal.
Mom was a tea drinker by taste, back then,
not yet having found the joy of a daily gin and tonic,
maybe two, depending on who's making – favouring
Dad's youngest brother Walt and his pouring hand,
who's counting, once a couple of gins in good company
in late afternoon didn't matter a whit for a widow past 65.

From the back of the cupboard our *Dziadek* brought out
one of his clear bottles with their florid enigmatic labels,
the liquid a harsh burn on Mom's innocent throat.

Across the white lace cloth,
all the kids watched Mom, highlight of the event,
as the little amber glasses were poured over protest,
and arms lifted in unison up to the center of the table
to clink, *na zdrowie*, and by Granddad's command
the drink went down the hatch in one.

Our mother's face screwed up just short of convulsion.
She coughed as if her father-in-law had given her
onions, varnish and nails in a shot
as a test or a private joke or a retribution.

But she took it for Dad's team every time,
paused speechless, shook her head,
cleared her shredded throat and sat down
to the comforting food, *good health* on platters
with sour cream on top carried from the kitchen
with Anna's hopeful little smile.

Sitting the Kids

Cousin Jim, six years older and our fierce protector,
would take us kids by the hand in a string of three,
point out our older sister—*Here's Felicia too*—
when people were fussing over the twins, make sure
when he was around we all got our care and due.

So our mother could go shopping unencumbered
by her active young three, a real treat, Jim naturally
was recruited to babysit us late afternoons
when he came for violin lessons across the street
at the Royal Conservatory of Music, Delta Branch.

Not much actual sitting.

He got closed into a coat cupboard way up in the attic
with no handle inside, being clever with hide-and-seek,
eventually had to bang and bash his way out.
We'd given up seeking, gone on
to other junior pursuits two floors down.

He got clobbered in the head by my brother Victor
taking a back swing with the bat in a baseball lesson.
Mom arrived home to her nephew prone on the couch
and us kids bringing him cold washcloths and kisses.

Not isolated incidents.

But he stuck with us through most of his teens
until we were ready to babysit the kids next door
for cokes, TV and a dollar, stuck with the adhesive
of flesh and blood, old ties and unassailable affection,
to his mother's eldest sister and her perilous brood
and also Mary, the girl he met down the street.

Dark Outside

Late one afternoon, I was about seven
with something of a cold coming on,
I went quietly to bed and slept through supper
and even later, waking in a dark room in a quiet house,
surprised it was so dark already, and where
was my mother who didn't wake me up to eat.

They must all be downstairs in the kitchen
finishing desert and tea or the dishes.

I wrapped myself up
in my long quilted dressing gown, the one
with the cherry lining and sash and meadow flower print
that my mom had sewn for Christmas,
tucked my doll under an arm for company
and headed for the stairs to get to where everyone
would be glad to see me.

One hand on the banister, one around my doll,
my foot above the first step down, I heard my mother
call from her bedroom, *It's the middle of the night,*
we're all asleep, go back to bed. Face turned
to my parents' door, I held my pose for quite some time,

foot in the air, considering how they'd gone on
without me, sinking disappointment,
not knowing whether to go down to no one there
or back to bed, and what if I wouldn't be able to sleep,
a pang of lonely in the night in the hall confused
and stuck, and when would there be breakfast,
and would my mother want to get up

with a squeeze and a few consoling words
or Dad come out to the hall with his violin
for a girl out of synch, but of course
he was 'dead to the world,' as our mother said,
and nobody moved or called again, and I stood,
even now uncertain where to go from here
and what to do with night.

Cribbage Lessons

My parents were known for playing cards.
The square padded card table got set up
at every family gathering, and the folding chairs.
You could kid around while you perused your hand,
considered strategy for maximum points
and hoped to confound each other,
raising howls of protest, "You son-of-a-gun,"
and delighted "Aha's" and "Gotcha's."
Personality comes out in a card game.

Dad's game was cribbage: one on one, two on two,
sometimes three lanes with "every man for himself."
He'd play with Mom if they were ever home together
with time on their hands, so hardly ever,
but they went out to play crib of an evening with pals,
and hearts and bridge with Mom's sisters.

Dad taught me cribbage just in time.
When I got skipped from grade two to four,
a popular idea in '40s grade school education
for the best reader in the class,
the smart kid was way behind.
Lost in arithmetic, messy at writing.
Worse than that, I had to leave my twin behind.
How can that come out right?

To add, subtract, divide in class, I did a lot of guessing
and parroted other kids doing sums at the chalk board,
glad to have Dad's good ear, but I was a nervous fake.
I'd also missed out on my joining of letters.
To keep up I printed fast and small like Dad, though
he printed like a draftsman, architecturally, and I didn't.

Dad taught me cribbage, and cribbage taught me math.
Every play required you to add up the value of your cards
on the spot, aloud, and Dad didn't let you dawdle.

I learned to glance along the board to peg in fives
and add points in my hand, calling the 15s and 31s,

the runs – Dad's eyes on my cards and mine on his.
Cribbage restored my dignity and my place in the class.
No such help with cursive. I'll always write like a lawyer.

...

For my mother on evenings alone I lay out solitaire,
the comforting slap of cards going down in the quiet,
and keep her pearls and wedding ring for her safely
as she asked at the end, who wouldn't?
But cribbage was my father's game and he made it mine
and I'm always ready to play. I'm known for it.

Bum to Bum

The double bed my sister and I shared
between our baby cribs and the twins we got as teens
was both a bower for girlish whispers and battlefield:
two growing girls without a buffer between,
though a board was often threatened, seeking space,
bumping kneecaps, flinging trespassing arms across
the militarized zone (there was no DMZ)
awake or asleep, bothering with cold feet

until in uncontainable exasperation
one or the other humped up on her knees
and turned to the metal headboard with the picture
of a basket of flowers, and laying the side of a hand
in the middle of the basket, she chop chop chopped
her way down the bed to define the boundary:
You're on my side!

This and the ensuing skirmish were not quiet.
But we ceased fire
when we heard Dad's slow footsteps climbing the stairs
and became two allies against the approaching spank.
Bum to bum, we whispered fiercely and linked arms
back-to-back in the harmony and good will
that settled between us over the bed, knowing

Dad home late from a shift and tired and sent up
by Mom would not be harsh as he pried us apart
to deliver one swat, swift and firm on each bum,
a bit of sting through our cotton pyjamas
from his hardened machinist's hands,
a whiff of metal and oil, just the one,
reluctant enforcer of the order of the house.

Maybe then, and sometimes instead, he'd pull out
his old violin, under-used and he under-practiced
and a bit out of tune but sweet to us all the same,
to sit on a wooden chair in the hallway
and, drifting with his father dreams, play us
off to the sleep we'd been resisting.

Perils Left, Right and Center

The old communicable diseases still dotted the 1940s.
They found their way to us and every home with kids.
Good thing our mother didn't go out to work,
she had her hands full with her little population
of three ready hosts for disease: *Wash your hands,
don't touch your face, oh hellelujah, not again!*

These came on top of infections that put me and my ear
in vertigo on the couch and sent my brother moaning to bed,
and my sister's bout with polio, which she fought and won.
No inoculations for the common diseases, not much treatment.
It was our immune systems and mothers against the invaders.

Mom brought cold washcloths for our foreheads, aspirin,
ginger ale, buttered toast, and chicken soup for all illness,
also scrambled eggs. Mentholatum rub or Vicks
on the chest under flannel pyjamas for a nasty cold,
and a dash of whisky and honey in hot lemonade
and to bed to sweat, to sleep, *oh do go to sleep,*
and maybe Mom could rest.

...

Three kids downed by chickenpox at once, two weeks
in bed with misery and itches you weren't to scratch
because you'd make scars. No contact with other kids,
schoolrooms depopulated, houses bursting,
much squirming and complaining.

My sister caught the measles, the hard red kind,
and had to stay for a week in our parents' bedroom
behind blankets that our mother rigged up on the window
against the light for her sensitive eyes and headache.
We read her stories from the doorway after school.
I wonder where our parents slept that week.

We twins got the milder faster kind of measles, Rubella,
and also the lumpy mumps. Mom went back and forth
between the kitchen and our rooms upstairs to calls
of *Mommy, Mommy!* and begged us to nap at the same time.

My brother also caught mono. Home for months
from school and confined to his room, one afternoon
he heard a screech below and looked out his window
to see our Boxer, Buster the car chaser and harasser of tires,
get run over in front of the house, one of those accidents
waiting to happen but not for a boy to see. But then,
our kitten got parked on, playing in leaves in the gutter.
Tippy with the white tail, Princess with none, we lose them.

I got exposed to pulmonary tuberculosis just from the air,
faced long institutional bed rest and appalling treatments,
but it seems my system fought it off, a self-inoculation.
My forearm swelled up from the skin test by injection
on everyone at our school, that's how we knew.
Masked nurses, angelic in starched white sleeved dresses
and winged caps, set tables up with needles and vials
on the stage where we had our plays and concerts.

There was a big gloomy TB sanatorium outside Hamilton
with its double-barred cross glowing red
where I held my breath passing in the car. I counted myself
a lucky girl when the X-Ray showed no damage to my lungs.
I will test positive for TB for life but never get it,
and Mom could at least drop TB off her list of worries for me.

Many a '50s teen got the cold sore virus
through innocent eager contact with other lips,
unaware it was forever, no one told us, not even
in grade eight health class where they taught us body parts
and not to have sex – references to VD veiled,
though the word got around – but we didn't even know
herpes' name, we just got it.

Perils left, right and center for kids.

...

In those years of marauding germs, glimmers of success:
cholera well under control, diphtheria, smallpox, mostly,
polio in '53, and even TB, medicine slowly methodically
advancing against the helplessness of parents,
who always halfway held their breath.

But neighbourhoods were safe for kids to play on our lawn,
Hide-and-Seek, Red Rover, Simon Says, Mother May I,
until supper was called.

Older, rougher, touch football right in the street,
a thrill for a girl who might forget and sort of tackle a boy
not her brother, and hockey. My brother played goalie,
wobbly for a forward, but my balance on blades was worse
from my unreliable inner ear—never could skate—
so with body checks also in the game,
I just jumped up and down on the sidelines,
learning to be a fan.

Safe to visit neighbours into winter dark by age 10 or so,
trusted by mothers to know when to get home for the night
and dodge the occasional flasher from the back ally.

Stomach Ache

My stomach didn't really hurt, well barely,
as I'd been known to overstuff myself at supper
on Mom's hearty cooking, but
I'd sometimes exaggerate
and tell my mother my stomach ached
just to stay home from school.
I suppose she knew.

Instead of the demands of the classroom,
I'd get to lounge in bed or on the couch
under a home-sewn quilt, and Mom would bring
me lightly buttered toast and Red Rose tea with milk
and lay her hand on my forehead
to check for no fever, no infection, thank God,
and that hand might linger and press and stroke
across my eyes and face,
the very gesture of care,
and I didn't betray myself and neither did she,
allowing me this once-in-a-while cheat.

Helen's Practice

"... to always walk tall and with a certain bearing, so people knew I meant business," from *Go to School, You're a little Black Boy*, memoir of Lincoln Alexander QC, 2006

Our Aunt Helen took a chance on her young brother
Ted fresh from law school and with a new wife,
both remarkably tall and smart and cordial,
and invited him into her law practice established
in Hamilton with first-generation determination
above Sobjeck's Groceteria on Barton Street, 619
near Ruth, the Blue Bird steps up the street for coffee.

She also hired her youngest sister to do research,
brains and beauty, our Aunt Joanne, and later on
our mother for capable reception and good cheer,
and Dad moved into an office upstairs. On weekends
he mopped the floors and toilets. It was family.

Helen had first made her way through Osgoode Hall
for training in law by serving summonses for the court,
riding Toronto streetcars to unsavory destinations
and hostile responses, did all the required, and at 23
was called to the bar as a lawyer and came back home.

But then the fight for work, one of the first
women lawyers in Hamilton, and the first Polish.
The Old Boys didn't seem to like either much,
so she opened her own damn practice, bought herself
a leather briefcase and a '42 Plymouth, two-tone green,
and after the war she took in her younger brother.

They formed the partnership of Okuloski and Okuloski,
Mówimy po polsku, the friendly Polish option,

Solicitors, Barristers and Notaries Public in gold

on the window where they settled at King and Sherman
by CIBC. QCs for Queen's Counsels were added in time.
Helen took estates and real estate, Ted favored corporate.

As Helen became known for being exacting,
all documents airtight, the wags among the lawyers
felt free to call them, fondly and with respect, *Oki & O.*
One of them thought Okuloski was Irish.

...

Enter young Lincoln Alexander,
newly called to the bar,
turned down over and over in his old hometown
for a job in law. Black men were rare in Hamilton then
and they were not lawyers.

Ted advised Linc: "Make your case to Helen."

Helen was the woman who rented a summer cottage
among the Jews at Turkey Point on Lake Erie,
brushing her hand at the *Gentiles Only* signs down the road.
And Helen had been through it with the Hamilton Old Boys.

She asked Linc for one thing: *Show me your credentials.*

Linc got the job, and Ted as a friend, and went on
to partnerships, his own QC, politics and official positions
– barriers and assumptions broken at every step –
to become 24th Lieutenant General of the province
while the Old Boys watched and the Okuloskis smiled.

In his retirement Hamilton named a new motorway
the Lincoln Alexander Parkway across the mountain
to join two ends of the city. Everyone calls it *The Linc.*
He found that both grand and amusing.
Lincoln didn't drive.

He came to Helen's funeral in 1993, and then
our family turned out, though diminished,
when he cut the parkway ribbon.
He had his chauffer drive him often on his road
and gave a grateful page to Helen in his book.

from *Diversifying the bar: lawyers make history*

Name: **OKULOSKI, Helen Frances**

Female
Born 1912 in Black Lake, Quebec
Died 1993

Called to the Bar:
1935
Q.C. 1955

Name of Heritage or Community:
Polish

Biographical Information:
Helen Okuloski was the first Polish lawyer in Hamilton and one of the city's first women lawyers

…

Helen, 1952

from *Diversifying the bar: lawyers make history*

Name: **OKULOSKI**, John Edward

Male
Born 1922 in Hamilton, Ontario
Died 1965

Called to the Bar:
1948

Name of Heritage or Community:
Polish

Biograghical Information:
Of Polish heritage, Edward Okuloski articled and then practised with his older sister, Helen, in Hamilton, Ontario.

...

Ted at Osgoode Hall graduation, 1948

Dad's Office

Granddad Okuloski succumbed at 60 to diabetes,
having drunk hard liquor as a tertiary occupation
through his adult life, depending on Frances, his wife,
to take up slack and endure drunken bouts, though
in business John bought judiciously, bargained fairly,
and he's the one who beheaded the Sunday chickens
for Grandma in the cellar and kept his eye on the orchards.
It was said in the family John Okuloski was a *decent man*.

He left behind at Barton & Barnesdale effectively a cabin
maybe 10 x 12, that we kids called "Grandad's shack,"
smack on the main street in the Hamilton Polish community.
The spot is now reduced to a slab of concrete, out of service.

Five-by-sevens of houses in black and white were stuck
on its windows and walls for his real estate agency,
which was second to his afternoon Polish chats
with the amblers of Barton Street, retired men
whose wives wanted them out of the apartment,
and who brought along a flask for the bench in the sun.

…

Two versions exist of why Dad left Stelco,
the Steel Company of Canada, in the 40s
and took over from Granddad when he died.

Either it was this:
Dad "spoke up for the men" with the boss
before there was a union and got fired.
Could have gotten somewhat heated;
Dad had Freedom Fighter in his genes.

Or it was this:
In the 2,000-man strike for 81 days in 1946
that brought the union in to Stelco, Local 1005,
our father crossed the picket line of angry strikers
every day and worked his machines as a scab.

He had five mouths to feed.
At strike's end, he had to quit. We were lucky
we didn't get paint thrown at our house.

Both sound like our father. Either way or some of each,
the Stelco job was gone.

...

Dad took over Granddad's business at Grandma's urging,
took it all, the listings, the tilting oak chair, the idlers,
the shack. A skilled machinist with a desk in a cabin.
Like many first-generation men, Dad turned entrepreneur.

He added insurance to the mix, Scottish Mutual & Life,
kept a sharp eye for listings and deals,
got out of the office to track them down,
fixed up fixer-uppers, dealt with tenants and toilets,
bought and sold, rented orchards to work the trees
for fruit, did clients' taxes,
translated for the court with exquisite Polish and English,
taking long hours away from home. Mom missed him
but that's the way it was.

When we got to 12, Mom took a job as receptionist
and office angel for her sister and brother, *at law*.
Dad moved out of the shack and south the few blocks
to their empty room upstairs, 760 King at Sherman,
to keep his papers and get to work on the phone.
Idlers don't drop by a law office, and it was a bit of a walk
from Barton Street. Besides, they'd have to get past Mom.

Humbly he mopped and waxed the building floors
after we teens gave up that dreaded family weekend job
and he drove a long series of Helen's cast-off cars,
one bright yellow that we called the *Banana Boat*.
Gone was his own shiny black four-door Ford,
cool knob on the steering wheel, gone his own choices.
But Dad was always up for a joke, and a way
to work things out.

...

In later years, he retrained as a machinist with young men
who called him "Professor," then worked in a small shop
until he got back on at Stelco with modest pay
and, this time, the Union:
Stelco Pass Number 18801, Clock 42133.
I've always thought of my father as a union man.

...

Through more thin than thick, our dad made us enough
for our sewing and books, all our stuff and shoes
—I never felt poor, just careful—
three Timex watches in our Christmas stockings,
in 1956 a TV, black and white and indistinct,
a pound of ground round every Saturday lunch,
and Sunday night a roasted chicken
and a cake in Mom's Sunbeam mixer.

Anything to Declare?

We weren't experienced smugglers
at the friendly border between Buffalo and Niagara Falls.
Not like my friend Val's mother, an early adopter
of Free Trade, who specifically drove "across the river"
to shop. The U.S. had the cheaper better cottons
but the tariffs were high.

She wore old underwear and a dress ready for charity
and dumped them in some department store Ladies Room
to return to Canada in two or three fresh layers,
"No, nothing to declare."

Dad took us kids one afternoon to the famous Buffalo Zoo
some 40 miles from home for the large exotic animals
and just as much the spun candy floss, plates of chips,
but you ordered "fries," wands with plastic streamers
for the girls, a pinwheel hat for our brother,
a stroll with our parents among the loud and lively cages.

"Anything to declare?" the man at the border asked crisply.
"A couple of sticks and a cap for the kids in the back,"
said Dad, gesturing with his thumb,
"and what they ate, about 10 bucks U.S.
It was a very good Sunday outing, thank you."

My mother maintained if you need to buy something
on a trip and you use it, like a forgotten slip,
it doesn't count for customs. Probably technically right.

But even though I know they'll be more likely
to look through my luggage
where I've conscientiously packed my purchases
separately with their tags and receipts at the ready,
I can't seem to go through a border
without giving a full and respectful report.

Musicals at The Palace

Our mother would be waiting for us to get
out of Memorial school at four on random Fridays,
unplanned, unannounced, unpredictable,
it was just an urge she had
to get out of the house and into a fantasy.
A mother's ample purse dangling from her arm,
she kept a sharp eye out to intercept us walking home.

We would pile excited onto the Hamilton trolley bus
at the Main and Balmoral stop, and each drop in our fare
for the 15-minute ride downtown to The Palace Theatre:
walk in any time, beginning, middle, end,
because the double feature would immediately replay
and you could sit through as many times as you wanted.

Musicals were the usual show, post-war optimistic:
On the Town, Oklahoma, Holiday Inn, Two Weeks with Love.
Sailors fell in love on a weekend pass in New York,
flashy Ann Miller the heavy hoofer, Gene Kelly dancing
from athletic thighs, out-dancing Fred Astaire in my mind.
Debbie Reynolds sang cheerful "Aba Daba Honeymoon"
on her road to teenage romance in her saddle shoes.
Some good lines in that song to annoy my twin, though
he didn't deserve it, *said the monkey to the chimp.*

Showboat, Kiss Me Kate, Seven Brides for Seven Brothers,
but my favourites, the sailors "on the town" dancing
in unlikely locations, bursting out with catchy tunes,
and how fast and sassy everything went
to an upbeat resolution,
everyone paired up as in a Shakespeare comedy.

The musical road to romance was rocky but short,
and it always turned out right for the girl in the end.
With Mom's penchant for revolving musicals
at The Palace and taking her kids with her for the ride,
I came to expect too much from romance and love,
but got pretty good at figuring out a story from the middle.

The Queen's Birthday

The 24th of May is the Queen's Birthday. If you don't give us a holiday, we'll all run away! **- Traditional chant**

We got taken on a hike every 24th of May,
one of our two annual "forced marches."
Dad field-marshaled us three kids and assorted pals
and sometimes our cousin Michele, starting out with pep,
south to the Hamilton Pressed Brick works furnace stacks,
Lawrence Road along the foot of the Hamilton mountain,
east to Albion Falls, just for example, he was inventive,
and I can't say how many miles, no one counted.

Unused to lengthy exercise, I a bit chubby, not fit
like Dad who worked machines and farmed,
our feet blistering under Band-Aids,
sweating into our neckerchiefs under the end-of-May sun,
abandoning left-right left-right left,
we kids were panting, wiping down our faces and necks,
begging people to let us drink from their lawn hoses,
staggering along for the pleasure of a day with Dad.

He cheerfully led us in marching songs, full voice.
Each of those "99 Bottles of Beer" had to fall
before we were done, and fair inventory was made
of the horrors at "The Quartermaster's Store" where
*There were rats, rats,
big as alley cats in the store, in the store. . . .*

We limped home to late supper and the pleased face of Mom,
who'd had herself a quiet day before the fireworks at 10,
and every 24th of May called on our Dad to repeat,
Hip Hip Hooray for the Queen.

The Catch

Her younger sisters, Helen, Rose and Joanne,
when they were all teens still at home,
just girls taking their best shot at the eldest,
the lanky pole vaulter with the straightest hair
many years before either was in fashion,
decided among themselves

that our mother should do the family ironing
because she had the biggest feet, just right
for standing all the hours it took.
She, as they pleaded their case to their mother,
was the most efficient and best for the job,
noting her thick flat thumbs, practically
an ironing machine with collars and cuffs,

establishing in our mother a lifelong suspicion
of compliments, both given and received:
a reflexive recoil – *Wait, what's the catch?*
She was also eldest daughter of a drinker
and there was often a catch.

Later on when she was a mother and wife
to be proud of and beloved in our house,
a mother who always showed up,
we wished we could magically erase
her resistance to praise.

Compliments were rare in either direction,
partly her way, partly the times,
though her cooking and sewing were safe ground.

But bragging about her kids
became our mother's finest art.
To the neighbours, the grocer, the ladies at the church
and over cards, she told all our best stories.
Call that compliment enough.

Pyrotechnics

The floor of our dad's garage was soft,
a fine gravel, almost black sand
like the others in our neighbourhood.

You could rake it up into your hands.
You could light a little fire
in the middle of the floor and feel safe.

Which is what we did, the three of us
at, say nine, ten, eleven, curious about physics
we collected paper matches in match books
from restaurants, bars, clubs,
carelessly set down by some adult

and made a little pile of matches
in the center of the floor
to watch flames burst and burn out
just a few inches and gone
on a boring Saturday afternoon
and tremble just a bit ourselves.

Until the day Dad came home early
from one of his rented orchards
in his big farm truck,
flung open the square garage door
and stared and scowled.

No more of that, get into the house.

Expecting far worse, we gladly ran.
The disappointment in Dad's eyes,
seeing his kids as budding arsonists,
took away the thrill, and there was
indeed no more of that.
No repercussions in the house.
Dad was good at keeping secrets.

Pass the Salt

With a shake of his hand upside down, Dad signaled us
to pass him the salt. Circling his finger around his cup
was his request for sugar or a refill or a teaspoon;
it took some interpretation. A soup spoon was easiest,
hand in a grip scooping upward to a silent slurp.
Without looking up from the folded *Hamilton Spec.*,
the classifieds, the local news,
Dad used pantomime as if words would distract him
from pursuing his business on into evening over supper.

Dinner was too fancy a word for us. *Dinner* meant you went out
dressed up and had a linen tablecloth and napkins
instead of paper serviettes. Like later at university with a date,
the boy picked you up, was paying and it merited some fuss.

Dinner didn't fit our daily kitchen table
with its oiled cloth hanging over the spindly dinette legs,
and everything went on the table at once, including the salad.
Even with the modern wood cabinets built by Mr. McEwen
from Nova Scotia with three and a half fingers on one hand,
and despite a proper fridge installed, "supper" suited us better.

Mom was expert at soups that were the definition of supper.
Her clear-the-fridge soups and her *kapusta* and her *barsczct*
were family legend, likewise the *bigos* that our Anglo Uncle Roy
called Hunter's Stew or more likely he said *pass the by-gosh*.
He had his fill on family fishing trips, wiping his handkerchief
across cabbage browned with *kielbasa* on his full black mustache.

Family casual, we were, and what the heck, we had no objection
that Dad was working among us instead of on a shift
or unplugging a rental sink or out pruning an orchard,
glad to have him with us.

He picked up his pencil now and then to circle an ad
with a long appreciative whistle,
and always complimented the cook as the kids got up to leave,
and then they talked about politics in their ward and secrets
in Polish and home felt good, even with homework ahead.

Quick at quips, he'd come out with a witty line
here and there to show he was partly listening,
and that was enough.
Dad tuning in and out like a Radio Free Europe
shortwave connection to Estonia
gave latitude for sibling barbed remarks,
an occasional friendly bump to a shin, a chat with Mom,
always mindful of our mime at the end of the table
and the next anticipated signal to his little kitchen fan club.

Pork on the Table

Mom got herself a modern oven with a timer she could set
once she went back to work, we could better afford it.
No slow cookers or frozen meals or microwaves in sight
in the '50s, and little time for making her soups or stews
or anything complex, so a roast became our weekday supper.

First thing she did with any meat brought home was salt it,
a preservation technique from the era of the wooden ice box
when a man in leather apron carried in the melting block
wrapped in canvas on his back, ice in the box for the week.

Salting was a necessary habit that continued after we got
the humming shoulder-high Kelvinator with its tiny freezer,
until the Loblaws came in at the end of the alley
and you could shop for a roast any day until 7.
Let the supermarket keep it fresh for you.

Loblaws also allowed Mr. Naylor to close his corner grocery
at Grosvenor and King and retire without
letting his regulars down. I missed him.
The Naylors lived above the shop and would come down
to the bell. You didn't have to take money to the store,
Mom had an account. He showed me how to wrap
a pound of ground beef or butter on the diagonal.

I also missed his butter. Who talked us into trans-fat
Oleo in a plastic pack you had to knead to get the capsule
of color distributed into the white glop?
Patriotism from the war or clever marketing?

When she took the bus home for lunch Mom
placed a roast in a pan in her oven set for 350 degrees,
turned the white knob, and click, it should start at 3:15.
She phoned home after school around 4:30, Liberty 56065,
from the office to check *did the oven go on, and please
start the veg, and set the table, will you, Dearie?
I'll be home soon.*

Never soon enough. Potatoes, carrots, cabbage,
and anything leafy that started out fresh and green
would be furiously boiled limp and soggy by the time
she got off the bus. Lacking finesse or smarts, we girls
didn't think to drain some water and let things simmer
until she came, or simply steam. Then we'd pour the potful
of boiled water into the sink, and there went the nutrients.
Would've made good soup.

...

My favourite roast growing up was pork. Dad had been fed
too much garlic as a kid—at school you could smell garlic
on first-generation kids from Central and Eastern Europe—
so no garlic in Mom's dishes, though I came to accept
the complex aroma from the exotic skin of the Hungarian
girl behind me in class.

As with all meat Mom used just "S & P,"
adding garden chives or dill, or parsley
clipped at the last minute by one of us for the potatoes.
From the supermarket, only iceberg lettuce.

Cruets of vinegar and oil on the table, good heavy glass,
and cutesy little salt and pepper sets we bought
for Mother's Day at Rankin's China Shop on Main,
where "Mad Man" Rankin rode a bull through rows of china
in 1949 to make his shop famous.

Over the top of the salty roast the expanse of skin and fat
was scored into diamonds. I'd have eaten all the crackling
on the carcass if I weren't competing with Mom.
Pork roast was surely why
I looked like a sausage in my Brownie uniform,
the leather belt making two vertical links of my stubby torso.

...

Mom provided as if food were running out,
but she had her reasons.
She was raised by emigrees from the Tsar;
her parents remembered life as second-class citizens

in occupied Poland, which is why they got out.
Born in 1910, my mother had lived through the scarcity
of two world wars and the Great Depression.
It made a mother nervous. Chubby kids
meant healthy kids, doctors said in the '40s,
and it had its sense and approval.

Mom's pantry and little fridge and tiny freezer
were always full, in case. Rows of tins,
meat salted, vegetables pickled, and all fruit
from the family acreage preserved with sugar
in the cellar for dessert.
Mom stocked us up like a Quartermaster.

I'd like to blame the Tsar of Russia, the Fat Cats
who brought on the Depression, the two World Wars,
also the margarine industry and pork for my girth.

And Eddy's doughnuts, yes please, I'll have a jelly.
Dad picked doughnuts up by the dozen in a pastry box
with bread late on Saturday afternoons for free.
Eddy so grateful to Dad his realtor for finding him
a good shop for a bakery on Barton,
he sometimes let us browse his kitchen.

Child of our farm and the minerals from Polish soil
in my grandparents' bones, I also love my potatoes.
Why was everything so tasty!

Gone Fishing

Give Dad a rowboat on Rice Lake soon after dawn
with his fiddly half-horse motor in back, the family
asleep in cottages on the shore, sunfish for breakfast.

Give him the River Grand feeding a Dunnville weir,
the rapids under the Jordan Harbor bridge,
lazy Grinder Creek out near the cemetery grounds,
a fast stream through the Mazurkiewicz farm while the kids
jump in the hayloft after country lunch, swing out on a rope.

Sometimes a quiet brother- or sister-in-law companion
by the splashing water at the foot of Elora Dam. Give him
rock bass, perch, pike, throw the carp and catfish back.

Give him a fishing pole and lots of line, a sinker, a spinner,
silver hooks, minnows from the laundry tub and a can
of morning worms from the lawn. Give him
a summer evening when the mosquitoes and other suckers
and nippers come out and the fish are biting,
an afternoon in fall, a halfway shaded bank and dry boots.

Let leaves flutter around his feet, the kids and dog nearby.
Let his son turn brown as he scouts for the flattest stones
or throws in a line. Let the girls loll with Betty and Veronica
and in between stories look up at the busy green world
and swat at bugs and gaze at moving water until hypnotized
and plop in stones and create the best round ripples
and try not to be loud and scare off the fish.

Let his wife be at home with a slow day and the radio.
Have sandwiches packed for all, a big thermos of milky tea,
then *foot-longs with the works* going home to give Mom
a break from supper, or maybe stop for lake fish and chips
wrapped in old news with vinegar, salt and grease.

Give him these, you'd be giving Dad his whistling songs:
his Verdi, his Chuck Berry, his Fats Domino,
his Green Door to his own Blue Heaven
and his kind of God.

Family Fishing, 1940s

Vic with Uncle Felix

Flo with young Florence

Grandma Frances, her nephew
Bronek and his Stella, c. 1965

Flo on a Sunday drive, c. 1960

Vic with Roy, c. 1964

Sunday Outings

At Elora dam, c. 1952

Polish Weddings

Our father got "walked around a few blocks" on Barton
at the end of weddings at the Polish Hall, Mom propping
his sagging shoulder and setting the pace and direction.

He was hardly a drinker, that's what it was.
But bottles of Seagram's 5 or 7 got set on the long tables
straight from packing boxes, one between every four guests
to start on, no matter your age, if you were tall enough.
Surprise, we put a small splash into our Canada Dry,
rye and ginger the party drink, and everything
called for a toast. Dad got pretty rubbery.

Utensils clinked on glasses, demanding lusty kisses
by the newlyweds while they tried to eat,
a couple of speeches by the men of the family,
thin slices of wedding cake heavy with fruit
to go under your pillow for dreams,
polkas and waltzes upstairs, and catching up.
Mom would watch Dad and call time to go.

But before we all got into the car, that walk around for Dad,
allowing his two girls a few more dances with courting boys,
the polka, the waltz. We were pretty good at those
by 6 years old and the dances stay in our limbs
like fluttering the Polish *R* off the front of the tongue.

Dad's mother Anna worked the evening in the kitchen
rolling softened cabbage around rice and meat, laying out
the *golumpki* in long pans, tomato poured on top,
gabbing her heart out in Polish to unburden herself
with the Ladies' Society of St. Stanislaus church.

She'd pause as she brought out the platters and sour cream,
in her hairnet with her apron pinned to her flowery bosom,
for a little smile at her eldest son pretending he was sober,
his foot-tapping wife, and her flushed granddaughters
leading the willing boys in a dance around the floor
after a couple of little drinks.

Fatherly Care

Dad was left in charge of the kids for two weeks
while Mom accompanied our Auntie Helen
on a car trip to cousins in Scranton Pennsylvania
and on south. Distant cousins who visited Hamilton
one August in wools, because we were in "The North,"
they sat melting in 90 degrees on Grandma's couch.

Dad in charge with Mom away, but a busy man.
He gathered the girls' hair into double ponytails
for the day with shoelaces wound around twice,
and that was pretty well our hygiene, plus clean teeth.
A bit dense and just short of fending for ourselves.

Lumpy porridge for every breakfast;
for supper, pork & beans from the tin,
and I can't think of how we managed lunch
after we ran out of the dishes Mom had left
and even the Habitat pea soup that our father sampled
at every café in Quebec in 1954. Beans, beans, beans.

Not a green on our plates, not a fresh apple.
Shopping was too much for our father
even to remember, and frying eggs.
The girls broke out in underarm rashes by day seven,
maybe pre-teen hormones, scant bathing, hot weather,
Dad's diet, missing Mom, or the whole list.

His son took a photo of Dad holding up a frying pan
with those beans black and stuck to the bottom,
vertically by the handle, not a bean dropping off,
Dad grinning at the classic mess he'd made of supper.
We were all impressed with the photogenic pan.

The trip itself was lovely for a mother away from the kids,
the open American road with her sister in socks and slacks,
riding in Helen's V-6, you can pass any car on the two-lanes,
late 50's motels and diners sprouting along the highways,
Helen picking up the tab to thank her companion.
But our mother didn't travel for awhile after that.

Herbs in the Yard

Putting the finishing touches on a supper,
Mom would sometimes send me out,
when I cruised through the kitchen,
to her little plot of herbs planted
right in front of her snapdragons and gladioli
by the compost pile at the back of the yard.
Roses and nicotiana scented the green picket fence
all night for my dreams as much as for passers-by.

Not being observant with plants,
though I knew a herb from a flower,
for the longest time I had to ask her to describe
which one she wanted exactly,
what kind of leaf, how tall, how broad the plant
or I'd risk bringing in a fistful of the wrong one,
though I came to like those fragrant moments
and went back gladly to the garden.

Mom mostly stayed simple Canadian with S & P,
but, say, in her *barczt* with pork ribs and sour cream,
some feathery dill was called for, and chives
should be snipped on tuna or egg salad
and newly dug potatoes.

The other herbs she planted anyway
were too exotic for Dad and rarely used,
marjoram, basil, chervil, culinary sage,
and complicated for me to identify
with my hopeless botany, though I tried,
my mind on imaginings and abstractions.

By the time I left home with a B.A., of course
I had simple chives and dill, curly parsley and bay,
mint, and most of the fancy ones down pat
and all my mother's favourite flowers and her ferns
and to my surprise I missed our fulsome yard.

Dad made us a see-saw there from a long board
and a big round of log, and that's where we played
tin soldiers and trucks on a mound of dirt, that's where
we had our birthday parties with neighbourhood kids,
and where you'd chat with Bessie over the fence,
where our dogs spent their daily lives and are buried
under lilacs, Buster, Tippy and Princess with no tail,
and then Brown with one lung from a lab at McGill,
and that's where I learned my mother's many plants.

Green Paint

Dad got quite a deal for himself "from a guy"
on some gallons of dark green paint.

He proceeded to paint everything green:
the fence all the way around our corner yard,
which took three coats, the gate,
the trim on the pebbled garage
and broad front porch and the wooden chairs,
window frames on our two-storey brick,
the dog house for Princess,
the cellar toilet room for 'the boys.'
Fortunately, not the kitchen woodwork
which he'd briefly considered
though the cans were marked "Exterior,"
but that was probably Mom.

He had a lot of paint. Could've been
enough for the neighbourhood, but no requests.
He took our teenaged teasing with aplomb.
Have a paintbrush, he said.

It was a heavy forest green, evoking even then, before
I'd ever seen such stands, generous ancient conifers.
Not the bright new green of spring, so cheerful,
but an old-growth green, comforting, well established,
like our father.

Paint companies have since come up with fanciful names:
Hunter Green, Essex, Back Woods, Black Spruce,
Salamander, Crocodile, Chimichurri, of course Dark Pine.
But the only name that ever comes to me,
no matter how many the years,
is what we called it as kids, Fence Green.

I see my own weathered pickets need painting,
scoured by hard rains, buffeted by salty winds
and it's spring. I'm thinking green.

Fireplace Demolition

The brick fireplace was in our dining room,
smoky and old. Bad plan, said Mom, who
liked to make a family dinner party now and then.
She took a sledgehammer to it with retaliatory swings
one afternoon while everyone else was out,
leaving a crumbled mess and no option for Dad
but to finish the job, close up the wall
and call in her Uncle Felix to put up paper.

Felix, who used to let us little girls comb his thin hair
softly as he sat under a reading lamp in the living room
and add barrettes, our sister Felicia named for him,
our great uncle with the sloping black coupe,

Felix brought his big book of samples in.
That one with the peonies, Mom pointed.
Dad's Uncle Jack would paint the other walls,
both men trading their three-piece suits and fedoras
for white overalls and painters' caps.

We used to hang our stockings there at Christmas.
Mom rolled her hair up around the bottom at the mirror
there before going out; I'd watch her like a little groupie.

We'd sit at the fireplace of an evening
in our Christmas dressing gowns
and warm our pyjamas, drink something hot,
Monday nights listen to Lux Radio Theatre at eight
as a treat years before there was TV,
and protest irrationally about going to bed.

But that time was well and done, we were
becoming young teens, out or buried in homework,
and she had a proper job. It was time for Mom.

Time to have her room the way she saw it.
Amazed to see our mother on this rampage,
who would object, not Dad, not us, she was right.
She also dreamed of wall-to-wall carpet.

Mom's New Carpet

Until the summer of 1957,
our living and dining room floors
were polished with socks.
Old-fashioned linoleum before we called it vinyl,
the floor got its periodic mopping from Mom
and then it was up to us three kids.

Our mother pulled out heavy wool socks
we hoped Dad was finished with,
and a big round can of thick floor wax,
solid like you'd put on cars,
and we skated around dispersing the paste
with our feet, working it in until we had a shine
and Mom called it good with warm buttered milk
for three and oatmeal cookies.

Came the era of wall-to-wall, and Mom was owed. She got
a soft silky light green carpet professionally laid down as if
she were dreaming. We hardly gave it more than a month.

You could say I bear the blame. The problem:
the carpet came the summer I found American Bandstand
on TV and watched them bop and jive. And it was Jimmy,
a boy my mother didn't like, older, dropped out of school,
fast, though we girls kept him in his place hanging around
on our porch, it was Jimmy who lead us into rock and jive
at young people's club at the church, a wavy blond,
he was slim, squirmy, slinky, don't trust his hands
with your heart, he knew the dance, it was Jimmy.

The girls called a party. Weekend of my sister's birthday
in October, her 16th after all, we had to, parents going out,
bunch of pals came in with cold pop and chips,
records from Elvis, Fats, and Jerry Lee on the stack.
What would we do, with our adolescent brains
and chemistry and all senses lit up like 16 candles?
It's a party, you flirt hard and you dance a little wild.
In your parents' living room. On the carpet.

The bop and jive had you grind your heels into the floor,
and Jimmy got us flinging and spinning around the room,
it's rock and roll tonight, girls and boys.

We left the carpet in wall-to-wall waves,
to be vacuumed next day of chips, and then
entirely re-stretched by the man who'd laid it down.
I'm sure we made our mother cry that night.
Sixty years later, some of us are still ashamed.

Death Benefits

If our ailing Grandma Anna hadn't died
three short months after Granddad Basil did,
her husband and her best support gone
in a Canadian world that never became familiar . . .

If Dad hadn't closed in the two broad porches
on the Maple side of the house, up and down,
in anticipation of her arrival to live with us, Anna
forlorn and confused from her empty house to ours . . .

If Dad's plan had gone forward to construct a bedroom
in the attic for us teen girls, and give our room
to his mother, perturbing to us but understood,
our adjacent second-floor porch to be enclosed
for our quiet grandmother to sit in relative peace—

our own porch where we kids had played our secret games
under the rustling maples and the silver birch on the corner,
closed the mullioned door into our bedroom for extra privacy
to play Doctor with the dusty attic medical books, and we
might crawl from the attic to sit forbidden on the roof . . .

If Granddad hadn't died and then Grandma so soon after,
well, to be blunt, my sister and I wouldn't have gotten
the new pink and grey flooring, the fresh paint,
the expanded room and new twin beds when all was done
at the perfect teenage time for girls to spread out,
not cram ourselves into the attic.

. . .

The new room gave us space
for a welcome second closet, our collection of shoes
and the skirts I was busy sewing,
the extended vanity discarded by Aunt Lois
serving as a homework desk along the broad windows
to gaze at the maples over geometry, history, Latin,
and up and down the street to see what was what.
So taken was I by our good fortune, I neglected to mourn.

Dad below in the 'conservatory' he'd constructed
from the matching downstairs porch
that had been an ample verandah for summer parties,
southern sun through the leaves,

to become his room for Sundays among Mom's ferns,
her faithful lemon tree, our bubbling goldfish tank,
to stretch out his feet in Romeo slippers
and the cushion-sole McGregor Happy Foot Socks
he got on every gift occasion.
His vinyl LP operas drifted upstairs as my father
whistled along to the soprano and the canary's joy.

You'd think I'd feel more guilt over my grandmother's loss
and our gain, as survivors tend to do, I knew I should,
but it didn't seem so bad. Until I wrote it down.

Song of the Birds

Our mother had a series of canaries singing solo
in a cage. One-two-three, she named them
Johnny, as if they were one bird and replaceable,
those reliable yellow songster boys
warbling arias to Dad's whistle of a Sunday,

enjoying wing-flapping baths in their anteroom spa,
shiny hanging toys with beads, and a swing,
cuttlebone for the beak, a mirror for company
and fresh seed, canary bliss, but each destined
one day to drop to the newspaper and gravel
at the bottom of the cage when he wore out—
and a new Johnny arrived.

For a change, Dad brought her a Java finch,
no melody, more a squawk from his curved red beak,
doing his best to please, he liked our chatter,
more like an exotic pet, he could almost do words
and ate apples and spinach. Mom named him Pal Joey
after the rogue from a play she'd seen with her sister
in summer stock at Niagara-on-the-Lake.

Joey expired in Mom's hand, to our dismay,
plucked from the cage for emergency nursing
after slumping on his perch.
I remember the picture, big black receiver
clutched in her left hand as she sought advice
and consolation from a neighbour on the phone,
the drooping bird held firmly in her right hand,
his eyes squeezed shut, giving up.

A drop of warm milk on the beak was her first attempt
to revive him – thinking to shock his little system.
Then a splash of rye, which brought his last squawk
and she almost dropped him.
Desperate treatments for a bird, but she was stumped
—and a mother.

Mom returned to her sweet singing Johnny
and Dad got back to Sunday duets,
though later on
a compromise budgie or two named Elvis
cheerfully twittered and warbled and squawked
all day to the pretty green bird in the mirror.

The Laundry Hustle

Mom's wringer washer was considered nice for the 1940s,
hoses attached to the taps on a cement double utility sink
where she also washed our dogs—with tomato juice
if they met a skunk from the alley.

Our clothes swished back and forth in the hot suds
in the little round white tub, then Mom fished them up
from the rinse water one by one, it took some time,
with a nicely turned laundry stick and sent each by hand
through the wringer so they came out squeezed flat.

Then to the double wicker basket ready to shake out
and hang on the line from the back porch off the kitchen.
I took the job I liked,
moving the clothesline along hand-over-hand
as the clean cottons swung and fluttered and hovered
over the yard and Mom's gardens, her herbs,
I thought, adding their scent.

...

We never glorified our cellar by calling it a basement.
It had unfinished concrete walls and floor
and a nearly bedroom-sized coal bin filled once a month,
a hill of coal poured through the chute from a delivery truck,
and the equal-sized fruit cellar on the other side
with all our mother's canning jars and pickle crocks
full for winter. The furnace reached its long fat arms
every which way to the heat registers in rooms upstairs,
like an octopus at gunpoint, I thought,
fed into warmth by shovels of coal from Dad
if he was home or Mom if not, until we got the oil tank.

Our mother spent more time down there than anyone else
in that dreary setting, sorting the clothes we'd dropped
down the clothes chute into the basket without thought,
and then the swishing machine and the whole rigmarole.

By the time we got to be teens Mom had done enough
and besides, she had a regular job, and announced
we kids would be doing our own clothes from then on.
She relented when I shamelessly pleaded our homework
and piano and social lives and futures, practising hustler
I was with my mother, leaving her unsure
whether to object to the con or admire the skill, or both.

OK, you'll do your own ironing.

But she got us thinking more realistically about the work
we created, especially us self-conscious girls.
That's when we took to "the nose test,"
inserting our notable family nose
into the garment underarms for a sniff,
that universal reassuring gesture.

Blouses and dresses passing the test
could be worn twice or more, if not crisp as before –
permanent press not yet invented – which cut down
gratefully on Mom's time in the cellar.
Our rumpled cottons were ahead of their time, though
the ironing board remained set up in the dining room
just in case we got inspired.

Mom had it right. Priorities change.
In time she was given a washer-dryer set
as a thank you from her employer and sister:
sort, load, set the dials; retrieve, shake and fold
onto the dining room chairs to put away, and done,
how modern!

Shat in Your Hat

Dad did a stint as foreman for a man
our family knew better than we sometimes wanted to,
a man set up in business by his more competent wife.
The job looked good for awhile.

But Dad saw the operation cutting corners and costs
on materials and methods,
playing loose with the written specs,
assembling a building
that wouldn't weather the years,
so he quit. Not quietly, not my father,
who took all injustice as a personal affront
and had to speak up, this was cheating.

He wrote a parting letter of resignation,
of disappointment, of distress, painfully
citing point by point what he'd seen done,
that ended like this:

You've shat in your own hat
and now you'll have to wear it.
I don't want to shit in mine.

Mom wouldn't let him send it.
We heard the kerfuffle in the kitchen.
Dad pared down the accusations, and cut the poetry,
the bitterness lifted from his chest just by reading
those words aloud in the kitchen to his wife.

Father and Mother Christmas

Dad went out after work to get his family a tree
on December 23rd as if we were in Poland. He was busy.
Every year, last on the block, from a lot on Ottawa Street,
discounted to a couple of bucks, sparse and skinny.

Mom whipped up the Ivory laundry soap flakes
with water in her mixer to blob onto the branches for snow.
Then we wound around the lights,
the big ones, green, red, yellow, blue, no white,
then from the cardboard box we lifted, hooked and hung
the coloured balls and oddities, some still left
from Mom's job at Woolworth's before she married,
in 1939 a penny apiece for employees.

Icicles next, stringing, winding, flinging,
filling in those discount spaces, we were
calling back and forth for approval, *how's it looking,
getting pretty good*, and Mom got on to the baking.

Finally the star on top, and the tree was dressed,
pronounced adequately fat and jolly to the eye, ready
for Christmas Eve, when, after all, the story says
the Magi set out on their camels from the East,
so let it be said that Dad wasn't really late.

Down from the attic too, solid wood Christmas structures
made by craftsman Uncle Roy, folk art for the family:
Santa popping out of a chimney, a waiting manger,
reindeer pulling their sleigh across the top of the piano.

The tree threw scented magic into our living room,
no matter its poor beginnings, and at night in my teens
until called to bed, I would sit with the tree
and Johnny Mathis for company
as it got into my dreamy head into the new year
when it went out to the sidewalk in a trail of needles.

...

For Christmas Eve, Mom made fried *chrust*, an eggy dough
stretched, slotted, tied in a knot, and powdered with sugar
like a fall of snow. My job,
to drop them into the sizzling bread pans of Crisco
on the stove until they floated golden on the oil,
retrieve each gently with a fork onto paper towels,
then shake the sieve of white over the top. Consistency
not required. Broken ones to the sous-chef, me.
Pile the pastries high on oval platters.

Happy in each other's way in the modest kitchen,
my mother beside me rolled, stuffed, pinched and boiled
the *pierogi* dumplings to take to Grandma's on the 24th.
A merry drink, a buffet, we picked up the family presents
in a carton for Dad to disperse next morning by the tree;
we girls had wrapped cousin gifts all day.
Just the one side of the family in play. Dad absorbed
into the robust gang of Okuloskis would visit his parents
maybe tomorrow.

...

With Granddad John gone, the dinner moved to our house
for good, and Mom was in charge of the Christmas feast.
Fetching, peeling, on kitchen duty, I had sous-chef's privilege
to commandeer the biggest hot raisin square from the pan
before the rest of the family came in, stamping fresh snow.

Cousins for the children's table with a durable cloth
that stretched well into the living room; extra leaves
at the waxed mahogany table for "the big people,"
all of us wearing something new from under the tree.

Dad worked the door and coats, and mixed drinks to order.
Cokes for the kids for the holiday.
A gin in the kitchen for Mom, heavy on the tonic, one ice,
Mom more Commonwealth than Polish in her drink.
She was the best cook, so everyone else
brought salads and sides and serious bottles.
Auntie Helen on rye would get squiffy and cackle.

Our godmother, Phyllis, who'd crossed the street at 11
with Christmas bread to go with our *kielbasa* and eggs

and presents in the morning, would start on the upright
with her rum. *So tired of dreaming of you,* she swayed
at Dad and he leaned in as if they had a little crush,
her notes sagging as she sipped, then on to Cole Porter,
party flat. Leave Christmas carols to the choirs.

Then Mom was the one to watch. Finishing in the kitchen
flushed about the time we had the table fully laid,
she slipped to her room to change into something red,
sweeping past the Christmas tree for wearable decorations.

Glass beads around her neck, a little tree ball hooked
with ribbon on an ear, something to make a garter,
a bit of jingle, unintended tinsel in her hair and her cheeks
warm and rosy from the oven and the rush and the gin,
her hair silver by her forties. Just so she emerged,
a real Mother Christmas arrived among us,
to wave her festive hand at the table, come sit.

Man From Manitoba

Dad had a soft spot for economic migrants.
His immigrant family had moved from Winnipeg
to look for work in the hot churning Hamilton steel mills
in the '30s, hard times, and it worked out for father and sons
at Stelco and Dofasco, pouring melted iron, fixing machines.
Dad also knew about sudden unemployment.

A man from Winnipeg called our number some 20 years on
asking for a bed for a few weeks to find work, get on his feet.
Dad put him up in the attic on a mattress. Never mind
that his teenaged girls or his wife might be perplexed
at this quiet man passing through the upstairs hallway
very early and late with just a nod, opening and closing
the attic door like a wraith who hadn't quite decided
whether or not to live. I remember his hand on the knob,
his dark hair and back, the sound of the door,
but not his voice or his name.

I thought about him lying on the narrow pad upstairs
with a blanket and a living room lamp,
and where did he eat? Not in our kitchen, he never
stopped to chat, and hardly used the bathroom.
The man kept his footprint in our house small and faint.

I wondered at his silence. Was it deference to us,
was it sadness at the loss that brought him here,
was it shyness, was it shame? But we let him be.

The man asked for a hand from Dad, and he got it
and his job and he shook Dad's hand
with a nod to Mom and he left.

Flying Feet

Our father slept in his boxer shorts,
which we called his *pantaloons,*
one foot sticking out from the covers.
My personal temperature control, he explained.
The left foot. He slept left of Mom by the door.

It was sculpted long, narrow and gleaming white
in muted morning light, like a piece of high-fired ceramic
and I admired the esthetics of that statuary foot
and thought it secretly aristocratic
as I tiptoed past his sleeping snoring form
with the bedroom door open for air –

quiet as if
he could be wakened when he was on night shift.
Our mother once had to crawl in through the coal bin,
destroying her party dress as he snored away, off shift.

I suppose I fell in love with those feet.
Feet I'd see soon after he came in around eight
sweaty from the machine shop and his trees and vines,
whipping off his Happy Foot socks in the hall,
whistling up the stairs on his way to the claw foot tub
and dutiful evening tea at Grandma's with Mom.

On those broad stairs I used to dream I was gliding down
without touching, he seemed to reach the landing
as if his feet were winged.

...

Our sweet little *Babcia,* blue eyes pleading innocence,
face a girlish round, white braids over her head like a tiara,
took to her couch soon after age 65
in the bungalow on East Main at Walter Ave.,
a follower of the soaps and bubbling Lawrence Welk,
to exercise Polish matriarchal privilege and pathos,
oy yoy yoy, my arthritis, my BMs,
her conversational filter gone leaky,

requiring our parents at her house with our aunt
for company most every evening of our teenage years,
late black tea and sandwiches, ham from the bone on rye
with dills from Mom's Mason jars,
Eat, you must be hungry,
leaving us kids to our homework and the prized TV.

Obliging man, Dad never put his foot down on her plan,
though he'd already had his long day away, nor did Mom
who had a second supper those evenings with her mother
– solidifying her softer rounder years
and for me, the image I keep of those disappearing feet.

The Singer

Meticulously picking up every fallen scrap and snip
of cloth and thread for the garbage can in the alley,
bundling the emerging garments upstairs
to the back of her bedroom closet, closing
the electric sewing machine, black with *Singer*
scrolled in fancy gold script, removing the spool of red
from the spindle and stashing her basket
before we burst through the door soon after 4 p.m.,

our mother sewed two little girls' dressing gowns in secret
before Christmas one year while we were at school,
and presumably the equivalent jacket for her son,
but I just remember mine, with the red sash.

On Christmas Eve we exclaimed over the largest packages
we'd ever received as presents in our seven and eight years.
Dad pulled them out from under the tree in the morning
playing Santa Claus while we ate twists of egg bread and fruit.

We put them on, and I danced around, the long skirt
brushing my toes, room to grow, meadow flowers
on the quilted print, silky cherry lining that swished,
reluctant to take it off for Christmas dinner, or ever, those years
as it got shorter, hem and sleeves extended once or twice
until I had to admit I'd outgrown it.

...

Without protest – I would have – she gamely made net tutus
for my ballet, slacks and vests for our brother's tap, costumes
for our school concerts, and she always dressed us up to go out.

In the black paper album with glued photo corners and ribbon ties,
the photos from before she married and became ours, in pictures
my daughter and I will scan this winter into the Cloud,
she was prettier than she ever claimed to be, and well turned out –
even when posed beside the family cow – and it must have stuck.

...

We considered our mother a pro. She sewed all the clothes
for three matching little kids, Felicia, Florence and Victor,
skirts and trousers with bibs, hounds-tooth wool capes for the girls,
a trimmed jacket with round brown buttons for Victor and a cap,
and I remember Viyella for shirts and pleated skirts with straps,
and as young teens, circular skirts over our net crinolines,
floating above bobby socks and saddle shoes

until my sister and I took the bus downtown
with enough in our purses for a dress from The Right House,
and Mom cut back. Our rack dresses seemed pretty clever
until the skimpy raw seams began to fray.

Our brother had no such demands, but we girls still got
our fantasy dresses from complicated patterns and difficult cloths
that we picked out for our proms – not thinking of our mother
fighting with slippery fabrics under the sewing foot,
taffeta, satin, chiffon, and in our many fittings bemoaning
the stiff bones to be built in to keep the bodice up.
She always said *I'll figure it out.*

Until her capstone piece, the long silver blue *peau de soie* gown
made for my high school graduation. I took the stage for a prize,
white gloves, corsage, my gown, flashed her a winning smile
and went on to dance in the gym with my date from McMaster.

That's when the black Singer that had done so much singing
got pretty well retired, used only for occasional mending
and letting out her sister's clothes to pack
for law conventions overseas—Mom the one to count on
among the four sisters, willingly. Otherwise,
the sewing cabinet became just a piece of furniture in a corner.

...

I learned to sew from watching my mother, and 8th grade
Home Ec., where I could never get the French knot at the end
of the thread, mocked by the teacher for my feckless fingers.
From Mom I got help – and her lifetime supply of Singer needles.

I ran my seams up too fast with my jumpy knee on the control,
like stomping on the gas of a V-6 without the skill to steer it
—not very straight—with my father's blazing impatience

to get it done, can't be helped, only fixed, as we both knew,
so pick out the thread with the hem ripper and do it over.

But I was my mother's child too, and a yard of cloth
could make a narrow pencil skirt for a curvy teen
and I could afford a nice yard of wool from summer savings
and learned to slow it down,
and it became my challenge and my pride
to appear in class with another new skirt on a Monday,
and let my mother sit back and consider what was to come.

1958 with Ken

Prom Dresses from the Singer

1959 with Marv

1960 with Val at Delta Secondary School graduation

Leander Boys

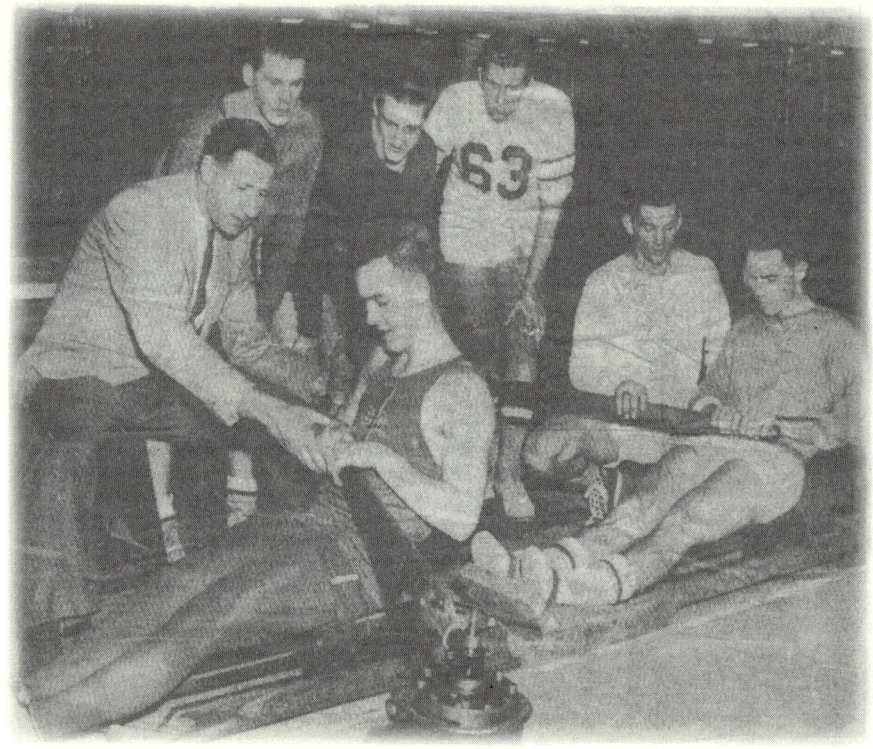

Claude Saunders gives advice to Pete Shuttleworth and Jack Lauder, young Leander oarsmen taking spring training indoors at Central gym. Others in the photograph include Don Morrison, Vic Skretkowicz, Joe Stempski and Ray Guy. Leander is seeking more young men for this year's crews including young fellows out of school and working. No experience necessary.

- *From the Hamilton Spectator, c. 1959*

Boy Meets Bay

Over several years, Delta High to McMaster U.,
my brother Vic came home in the long light evenings,
head high on his thickening neck and shoulders, but
suffering angry blisters on his palms from wooden oars,
the worst of his team, and once in a while
bearing the notable smell of industrial waste.

Not quite stinking, you wouldn't pinch your nose,
as he'd had a shower at the boat club
and changed his clothes,
but there was a lingering odor left
in his leather gym bag and on his skin
as he strode in, halfway alien in the expectant house.

It was the bay. The steel mills that gave Hamilton jobs
had been adding to the soup at our western tip
of Lake Ontario for decades. Out in the narrow racing shell
he also saw the occasional piece of something human
floating close, toilet paper being the clue.

Victor was an oarsman with Hamilton's Leander Boat Club.
The single scullers, lightweight fours and heavy eights
practiced most every summer evening.
No one wanted to fall in.
An upset, a dunk, and boy meets bay,
close your mouth, hold your breath and don't linger.
Mom was glad by then we had the washer-dryer.

...

Victor had fallen from a boat before at six or seven, fishing.
Dad reached his long arm down from the rowboat to haul up
his son while the boy gazed around at the wavering green
world under water, wondering if it could be a lovely option.

At 10 he had some useful early practice with sewage,
hunting frogs with young cousin Michele from Red Hill
past Mount Albion Road, two game little stalkers
venturing a little beyond permission.

Like his father, not much could stop him if he had a goal.
He dared himself to walk the edge of a big storm sewer,
stagnant and foul, and our boy tipped in and soaked it up.

Aunt Joanne drove the odiferous mess home on towels
with windows down, no scolding in the crisis,
but no more pleased with her nephew at the moment
than his mother was with her son when he was unloaded.

Clothes straight to the concrete sink in the cellar for a rinse
and then the wringer washer, extra suds,
and a bath for the sorry boy in the clawfoot tub
with red Lifebuoy soap, emerging carbolic
but embraceable again, wrap up your son.

...

The crew of Leander oarsmen might take a little dip
after a summer race at the Royal Canadian Henley Regatta,
a trophy for the mile in '58 for the Delta four.
For sure they'd toss the winning coxswain in.

Clean, Lake Erie then, and bathwater warm, fit
for champions Andreychuk, Shuttleworth and Stempski,
young Skretkowicz too with blue dreaming eyes,
all strong and supple and shy for teasing,
just ask the girls, and his two sisters, who cheered
his progress to Oarsman of the Year for his club,
could see the man their brother was becoming.

Tax Night in Canada

Approaching midnight, April 30th of every year
my dad would sit in the crawling line of cars
at the Hamilton Post Office downtown waiting
to get his tax return envelope in the mail
and post-marked on time by Canada Post.

For half of March and all of April
our mahogany dining table for eight,
and more with the leaves, was taken over by stacks
of other people's papers and receipts in boxes
as, evenings after work, lips tight, pencils sharp,
cups of tea, maybe a single Red Cap ale,
as his youngest brother worked for Carling's,
Dad sorted and figured and filled in
his clients' tax returns, setting his aside for last,
which usually meant the very last day,

which put him in that line of idling cars
and exhausted citizens fulfilling their annual duty
to Ottawa and Toronto, running late,
a sure sign of Spring.

Opting out of online filing and H&R Block,
though my tax drink is sherry,
and maybe it's a tribute and maybe it's genetic,

I continue the ritual of figuring my sums, of pencil
on paper forms from the library at the dining table,
of envelopes and extra first-class stamps
and the Post Office visit downtown close to deadline

to remember my father, as if beside me,
though never quite so late
as tax night at 11 when the cars wait in line.

Must Have Been Moonglow

Dad's long thick lashes swept against his lenses.
He kept a handkerchief handy in his pocket
to wipe the smudges from the glass.
I imagine women envied him, or fluttered.

His lenses, completely round long before
that was cool, the thin wire frames and stems,
supported the insouciant image of "the old man,"
which our handsome father fostered
from the time he turned 40.

They evoked a tease from us teenage girls.
We called his glasses his *Moonglows*
and hummed the song by Tony Bennett.

Dad was the perfect man to tease
because he liked it when his daughters saw him
well enough to make a running joke
about the character he was playing,
knowing it was exactly who he was.

Good Shot!

Dad and I enjoyed a good hot discussion,
especially at extended family gatherings,
get a couple of uncles and cousins involved,
a bit of socio-political rowdy by the fireplace
over a Seagram's or tea after dishes were done.

Mom would call them arguments,
and as Dad's voice went up the scale
and there was volume, she'd call out,
Vic, Vic, your blood pressure,
as his readings indeed were a bit up,
and Dad would oblige, sit back, sip his tea.

But not before a look across the room,
our conspiracy of two, to recognize between us
that we were of a like mind, and he'd gotten off
a couple of pretty good shots worth shooting
before the health inspector caught on.

Winter Coats

We began to refer to our lawyer aunt as *HFO* in our late teens,
the way she signed her name. In conversation, maybe *Helen*.
Whatever happened to Auntie? she wailed at us one evening,
propelling us right back to *Auntie Helen* for the duration.

In those middle years, say either side of 50,
Helen took to wearing fur in winter, especially her long mink
when she drove the 35 miles east to Toronto on the Queen E.
—more *Helen* and *HFO* than anybody's Auntie –
cigarette in the V of two fingers, slow white exhale,
the lady extracting pleasure from her occasional smoke,
wide play in the wheel, pumps on the pedals, coat undone

to meet up with a *gentleman friend*
she wasn't going to talk to us about. She could afford
the mink and the summer storage, the gossip, and the gas
for her sequence of new V-6s with sweeping lines.

Helen was a stunner at the train station on James St North
leaving for law conferences overseas year after year,
her favoured way to see the world, by tax deduction.

Wardrobe amended and packed by our mother:
a 50s travel suit, alligator pumps and handbag, maybe a fur,
hair permed under a tricky little hat, suitcases that matched.
Her family of cheerful luggage bearers, embracers and wavers
called out *bon voyage* for exotic travels.

...

My mother and I went with her to shop for her mink
one Saturday at Eaton's in Toronto on Yonge, the posh salon
on an upper floor reserved for coats. You couldn't browse
the furs, they were brought out one at a time to consider,
taken out from under wrap on long-necked wood hangers,
no pawing the goods, ladies, and tea I believe was served.

Helen did look *downtown-Toronto* in every coat she tried on,
wrapped in winter animal softness. It does something
to a woman's face; a man would want to offer his arm.
The best ones got a spontaneous twirl.

She bought a long brown coat of lush warm female pelts.
As later did my sister, working at a hospital in Montreal.
She cashed in her Canada Savings Bonds for the coat,
she was freezing! You really have to up there, she told us,
Laurentian winds blowing snow through the streets
at 30 below, and women who dress up for the city.

...

Hamilton jest domem: my souvenir T-shirt from cousin Jim
declares. Hamilton *was* our family home.
Chilling but bearable winters. The wait at night
for the city bus wasn't so bad if you jumped around,
snow powdering our kerchiefs and coats, frost at our toes.
We objected to weather below even Fahrenheit 20,
though the Polar Vortex has shifted that perspective.

We were Canada's steel city during and after the war,
three mills with steady jobs, neighbourhoods of small houses
in brick from the local brickworks at the foot of the mountain,
lunch buckets, thermoses and weary faces
on the bus at the end of shifts.
Sports fans call Hamilton *The Hammer,* a nod to its grit.
It was a town for blue collars and warm wools.

At department stores winter coats came in serviceable weave
with warm chamois liners, cut to go over extra sweaters,
almost warm enough for the bus stop, and good enough
for sloshing home in galoshes from Grandma's along Main
when Dad's car ran out of gas halfway at Kenilworth.

Navy and brown for kids and teens didn't *show the dirt,*
but for the careful or daring there was camel hair with a belt.
Lots of black for adults: black for sophistication,
black for the dirt, black for the long lamentation of the old,
for all the grandmothers come from Eastern Europe
with wool flowered scarves tied over their heads.

...

From my mother, I inherited Helen's curly Persian lamb,
light grey, long to the calves, with wide lapels
– stored in my attic in plastic on the north Pacific coast,
unneeded. Helen wore it often to the county courthouse.

...

Heavy on the shoulders, the lamb, way too much coat.
Women in my family bought their coats oversized
to accommodate a suit underneath, the suit jacket
already cut big enough for a bulky sweater.

Helen's blond mink swing jacket also languishes upstairs,
large as expected, the pelts in the yoke splitting from neglect.
My sister keeps the two long minks at home,
hers and Helen's, as safe as savings bonds.
In winter they warm her feet at night and dress up her bed.

I'm not custodian of Helen's brown mink stole,
which went to a helpful neighbour of Mom's in 1994,
so it's had a better chance of surviving in good shape,
the one my mother borrowed for extra-special occasions
and wrapped around me for my McMaster graduation
in 1963, escorted by Dad,
and I wrote my aunt a thank-you note for use of the stole
and for the customery crisp twenty tucked into her card.

...

The borrowed stole aside, the closest Mom got
to a mink or fur of any kind, until Helen died
and left hers behind, was in that Eaton's salon,
approving and disapproving coats for her younger sister,
draping them one-by-one over her arms,
and she was called on to organize the cleaning and storage
thereafter, her hands smoothing the soft sleeves and plackets.

In a surprise drawing that Saturday afternoon at Eaton's,
lucky girl, I won a tomato-red wool coat with rounded collar
and a swingy cut, a happy, easy coat on into my 20s.
My French professor told me I looked like an autumn leaf
floating around the McMaster campus.

So who wants a mink or a Persian?

Hallway at Twilight

Motivated by the last-minute rush,
I often pulled an all-nighter at the kitchen table
for some university exam or other the next day,
milky black Red Rose tea from Mom's Brown Betty pot,
sometimes with my studious brother across from me
who didn't have quite so much left to review,
and could reasonably close his books and go to bed,
but we liked it while it lasted.

About the time I set my books aside, rinsed my cup
and headed for the stairs, the early sun about to send
its light blue hour through the windows, that's when
my father would be getting up for his 7 to 3.

We'd meet in the upstairs hallway
headed into and out of the bathroom,
he to the kitchen and I to bed
for a couple of hours before class,

to exchange wry smiles at the change of shifts
at our house. And then we shook hands,
just the one firm shake,
pleased as if we'd planned it and kept a secret.

He was my "good morning" and I was his "good night,"
and no more was said.
Seems now like not very much, but it was.

Toilet in the Trunk

For several months in 1963, our father kept a toilet in the trunk
of his car. I'm not saying a toilet seat. An entire toilet,
white ceramic, waiting to be installed at one of the fixer-uppers
he'd spot in the nightly classifieds to do up, rent out or sell on,
not telling our mother so he could reinvest in the next project.
She'd find out when the tenants called about a leaky toilet
and they'd give us a new address off Barton or Cope.

He had this ambition to set them up on some acreage
in a ranch-style house where he could have orchards
of his own and she could retire to her garden,
and his deals would get them there.
Meantime, he kept his wife guessing.

...

In 1963 my summer job for HRD required a car
– supervising playground programs around the west end
in my crisp white shirt and tan and frosted hair–
so Dad let me use the big blue Chevy with the fins,
like driving a couch, and he used his farm truck.

Dad's toilet went with me. In the trunk,
riding low. A couple of times off road.
I kept my supervisor manuals and files and purse
on the back seat under a blanket,
because what young woman in 1963 wanted
to open the trunk onsite to expose a toilet to her staff
and all the playground kids? Now, I quite like the idea.

The toilet accompanied me and my friends every chance
we could get the car – once as far away as Georgian Bay.
Dad never asked about the mileage or the gas.
We allowed each other our peccadillos, fair is fair.

The toilet tagged along, a comment on all proceedings,
a lesson in humility, burdens and secrets gladly borne.
Pretty sure we never told Mom.

No Spitting

Stopped for the light at King and Gage,
my father spits a spray of cherry pits
out the window of his farm truck
from the pony basket on the seat beside him
which he's been chewing through en route to work,
pouching the pits until he's got enough
for a good shot, and easily missing
the turning cars with his practiced aim.

"But they're natural," says Dad
as the cop writes up the warning.
"It's the 3 to 11," he tells me later,
"I can get away with it on the night shift."

Don't Go!

My father didn't want me to go to Minneapolis
for a Ph.D. in 1966. The University of Minnesota
would take me into the heart of America
and someone or something in America
would win my more-than academic heart
and I'd stay past my student visa and make my life.

So he took the old slow highway to Toronto airport
in the powder-blue Chevy from Helen with 60's fins,
Lakeshore Drive parallel to the hectic Queen E.,
the scenic route along Lake Ontario, driving 40 tops,
to remind me how lovely a place we lived in,
and I was last on the plane, with a hasty wave back,
he was right.

To Have Girls

As an adult I wanted to apologize to my Dad one evening
on a June Greyhound visit from Minnesota as we walked
the furrows at one of his rented orchards after work,
pears and plums, I think it was, Dad happy in his boots.

Tried to apologize for all the maddening inconvenience,
the frustration, grief, loss of hair, gritted teeth
I'd caused him in my teens,
though it did make him an expert whistler.

Sorry for:

Tying up the phone line with teen gossip, giggles, guffaws,
our voices muffled behind the winter coats in the closet,
so that in a proper fury
he installed an identical second phone
with its own line and number on the wall
six inches from the first big black dialer, Liberty 56065,
two phones lined up, messages to be penciled on the wall,
to let his tenants and clients and himself
for God's sake get through!

A man who whistled sweetly and played a bit of violin
in the upstairs hall at night when we couldn't sleep,
or pretended,
his upset got directed at solutions, not his girls,
who on teenage time, felt guilty for maybe a week.

Sorry too for:

Tying up the single bathroom with girlish mirror posing
and supposing so that one afternoon Dad banged together
a toilet room in the cellar by the stairs, let's call it .25
of a bathroom, just the toilet, no door, for the boys,
not pretty, bare studs, wash your hands in the laundry tub.
The Foo Room painted in green over the open doorway,
handy beside my teenage brother's darkroom,
my friends and I willing models for his camera practice.

Next would be outrageous necking on the summer lawn
with random dates, already pretty late getting home
and Dad sent to the porch lit-up by Mom to call me in.

I'm sorry.

Dad held up his hand against the list.
That's alright, he said, his face going dreamy,
and I thought of times he'd taken us fishing
and he let me float my plastic swan around on a string
instead of handling and piercing wriggling worms,
my reckless hair he roughly tied with shoe laces
in bushy double foxtails,
and in my last year at home,
our eager dates for foreign films at Mac in winter coats,
no evening orchards calling him away
—tender times like these—
and I think so did he.

Nothing, he said, to his grown-up daughter, me,
there's nothing so sweet as having girls.

Hop In

Mom and Dad drove me west the summer of '69,
Ontario to Michigan, Indiana, the corner of Illinois,
returning me to my waiting husband
at his parents' big split level on Chicago's south side,
the in-laws having a weekend together
at the end of my few days' visit back in Hamilton.

As my parents got into the car after the goodbyes,
my mother held the rear door open.

Hop in, she said to me, the way she did,
and because I didn't, it dawned on her then,
even though she already knew, she didn't really,

that I was married now and lived in BC
and would be going on west
as they retraced their tracks in the other direction
and it would be a long ride home
to Hamilton without her daughter.

The Winnipeg House

The old house in Winnipeg was gone
by the time Dad and Mom got off the bus in 1970
for a look as they crossed Canada westward
to visit me at UBC on the coast,
the house where Dad had lived into his teens
until the family of five packed up for Hamilton
and work in the steel mills some 40 years before.

Deemed an eyesore? Condemned for its imminent collapse
or urban renewal? A flight to the suburbs? Force of nature?
Too late for him to ask.

But here was the place, and he could almost see the house,
the way your brain might tell you the top of Mt St Helen's
is still there, until you remind yourself, no, it's gone,
shake your head, rub your eyes. Traces left behind
like people who used to live in your heart now lost
but not, that's how he saw the house.

We're standing on the front porch, he said,
and over here was the kitchen, and right there my bed,
and all the rooms where he'd spent his early life and left
and he now stood.

...

To return to your first house from far away
settles an old persistent longing.
Like salmon who recognize the very stream of their birth,
your bones know they're standing where they started.

I go back now and then to our old indelible corner
and see the red brick house on Maple as it used to be,
filled with us five, not the up-down duplex it became,
and consider time and place and choices we have to make.

...

So it was enough for Dad, that day, just that grassy lot
with Mom alongside. They had another bus to catch,
two days and a thousand miles more to get to their daughter,

the flattened prairie Dad would see with new eyes,
all the lakes, and Mom never west or north of Georgian Bay.

And then the Rockies, the Rockies ahead, foothills, glaciers,
jagged peaks, gasping drop-offs, thickness of ancient trees,
photos of Mom to take, their first wild Pacific fish,
a Chinatown out in Vancouver, all to the storied West

waiting beyond this stop at Dad's old house
where Mom gave Dad a squeeze and he raised his hand
farewell and they left for the station.

Tickets safely in Mom's purse for the cross-country ride
back home on the train going east. They could raise a glass
to Winnipeg when they passed in the dining car
as a last goodbye, she said, *let's get going.*

...

Along the way they'd find two paintings in a gallery
out of Yoho Park, the only art my parents ever bought,
an impulsive buy for the sake of the happy trip.

Hers, a high mountain range embraced by evergreens,
snow and sun, and his, a dark lone pine bending
over a shaded lake at dusk, as solitary pines
will lean from prevailing winds,
to hang them side-by-side over the couch on Ridge Road
at home, and those in time would come back west to me.

Night Road in Montana

Antelope leapt across the straight flat highway constantly
and countless deer turned their high white tails on the run
so they had to dim the headlights and slow to 35 or less.

It was like a story my father had heard of the West
but never thought to see,
right in front of him and left and right
this enchanted rural scene etching into his mind
over the hours they drove that night,

Dad keeping company with my husband on the road back
from a ceremony at the Lakota Res in the Dakotas, back west
to Mom and me waiting in the Bridger Mountains of Montana
where I lived with Paul,
two men in a dreamscape, a night my dad would never forget.
They arrived in the morning with faraway eyes and bleary.

On the drive east to Ontario and the machine shop and farm,
Dad bought himself a black 10-gallon hat in Wyoming
at a highway tourist stop
to wear when the occasion called for something special
or he just wanted to keep the thought
and count himself *one lucky son of a gun.*

You Deserve It

In his very last years, when all Dad's efforts
were paying off and he got to ease up,
and he had just as much reason to say it to himself,
he took to telling Mom, when something nice
came her way, *you deserve it!*

Not the accusatory meaning in common parlance
that we were cringingly accustomed to: *you
brought this down on yourself, you know, you deserve it.*
No, it was purely, sweetly said by Dad,
and he meant it, *you deserve it.*

He came to say it to others who weren't so sure
of that essential truth, and I was flabbergasted
and touched and tearful when he said it to me
just when I needed such a mantra, *you deserve it.*

No begrudging that the words hadn't come sooner
to his lips. Men didn't talk that way back then,
but somehow the words came to my father
because that's the way he wanted to be, in the end,
and they came in time and he deserved it.

Pork, *Not So Much*

It might have been the pig farm upwind that put them off
or maybe they just began to think of their arteries
and Mom had the time and pleasure again to cook
or all of the above, but the menu changed at Mom and Dad's
when they moved to their new brick ranch up on Ridge Road
and Mom retired at 60.

Slow and healthy soups and stews came back to the table.
Out the picture window a view of Dad's tractor and ladders
among the fruit trees and the leafy rows of Mom's plantings,
no garlic, but onions and everything else you'd want to grow.

Under the table the former stray dog I named
pretty girl *Guapa*, though she was not,
and brought home to Dad from Toronto streets
waited for action by his brown Romeos.
Five black cats hunted the nine acres, followed Mom,
and napped sleek on the couch, also my doing,
a surprise litter from my young Siamese
picked up in our laundry room in Vancouver
and knocked up in Chicago on the trip over, oops.

On the table Birks' Mother's Day sale dishes,
Brown Betty teapot and the stainless tableware
– the best silverplate still kept for parties –
and at his place Dad's pencil and classifieds
from *The Spec,* front section for Mom.
Roast pork on the table, no, not so much.

...

In the third generation born in the '80s, my girl
would confound her Granny at the age of seven
by going vegetarian: *But how can she eat no meat!*
My now-vegan daughter uses a pile of pans
for photogenic dishes made with panache
and entire heads of garlic that would choke my dad.

At my house it's mostly Northwest. Wild salmon
from Alaska or the sparkling tidal bay across the street.

From nearby farms, organic veg sauté, oven potatoes
with a touch of butter, a heap of salad greens.

Many a Sunday I roast a chicken, that family tradition,
though I don't keep the bird alive overnight in the cellar
from the Saturday chicken man, as Grandma did
before Grandad went down to wring its neck.
Pork hardly ever, though in a taco—OK!

But comes a holiday, my mouth wants to be Polish.
Cabbage rolls full of meat and rice
from the Romanian café will do, pickled herring
from a jar at Costco makes me a good Christmas Eve.
Omit the *studzienina*, Babcia's jellied pigs' feet.
Barton Street *kielbasa* in my dreams. But hey,
potato-cheese *pierogi* do come frozen, ready-made;
I'm lazy and accept the stiffer dough.
Skip the pork suet on top, pile on browned onions
melted in butter, and I'm good. I mean, they're potato!
Prosze, pass the sour cream.

...

Pour a glass of white wine for me and my girl
—remembering those sweet Niagara grapes—
a large G&T for Mom – one ice for a Canadian lady.
One Molson's Blue for Dad, thank you, *dziekuje*.

Toast *na zdrowie* to your health, all the Dearies,
to our good life, and good night, *dobranoc*.

Call Me

We called him Daddy, we called him Daddy-o,
we called him Moonglow, we called him Dad.

Call me anything, but call me,
he often said.

Wish I had.

Out of the Nest

Vic with Florence, McMaster University graduation, 1963

Kids' visit home from Montana, Montreal and Scotland, to Ridge Road house, 1973

The Machinist

Vic at Machine Shop, 1970's

For the Future

Dad planted hundreds of cherry trees at the bottom
of his nine acres at the ridge of Hamilton mountain east
above Stoney Creek ON in the summer of 1975,
his last as a farmer.

These apart from his established trees in rich Niagara soil:
plums, pears, cherries, apples and peaches eaten fresh
off the branches or jarred by Mom the gardener
and her tomatoes, potatoes, berries, cukes, and other greens
tended and washed up for lunch and supper or given away.

The extra fruit Dad drove in his farm truck down Highway 8
to the jam factory E.D. Smith's by Winona, including grapes,
whose vines he learned to cultivate latish in life
from Augustino Carpani, Auggie at 90 and more at the time.

When Smith's deemed several bushels "wind spoil,"
bruised by a heavy wind up on the ridge, Dad kept those
for his grape or cherry wine that made everyone flinch,
best drunk in the cellar with Dad in one aspirational go,
na zdrowie and clink the little glasses and laugh.
Nephew Jim turned some wind spoil into heavenly wine
and sent Dad two bottles that intoxicated him completely.

...

Given the size of the baby trees, the grunts, groans and sweat
and the long labouring of the tractor,
our practical mother exclaimed to her dreamer husband,
*Vic, why are you doing this? You'll never live to see
those trees grown and producing.* Which meant: *Vic,
come in and spend the time with me instead of your tractor.*

In a lifelong dedication to avoiding misfortune
our mother was one to caution people about their perils,
her warnings flying behind us like scarves as we ran
to our fates, and she started early on their demise.

Let's note that, though he enjoyed playing the old man,
my father was a hardy 59 at the time.

He got the point, but he planted the trees,
maybe knowing in his way that he wouldn't
quite see 61 and this was his chance.

I don't mind, he replied. *They're for the future.*

The trees, the new apiary, the organic farming magazines
he was almost ready for another way of farming

– the future –

when the toxic industrial sprays got to his brain
and none of us in any position or mind to take over,
not Mom at 66: *No 60-year-old woman should be up a tree,*
she'd declared when she quit the orchard.

Mr. Carpani came to pay his respects. As did some widower
unknown to us, pursuing Mom and the farm, a reader of obits,
whom she sent away without the drink or lunch or date or farm
he expected. He turned from gazing at the coveted fields to stare
at her face in the sun for a sign and asked my grieving mother
bluntly in Polish, *But Mrs., where are your wrinkles?*
Never mind him, he didn't get past the patio.

...

Those of us left today, we all wish, everyone would, the best
for the kids of the brothers who bought the farm together in '78
at a quick-sale price, excited young men answering the sign
I banged up for Mom by the road, *For Sale, Inquire Within*
– something Dad would've done – and the right people came.
Mom wrote up a kind contract, soft-hearted as she was
toward such nice family men who would farm the land
and had sons to follow, still living there all these years along.
Well done to Mom.

We who joyfully knew those tender people who came before,
we do fervently hope
that those kids and their kids after them keep tending the bees
and pruning those trees, and eating the cherries with abandon
and glorious spitting of the pits, all with the best organic method,
everyone and the land safe and healthy and fruitful,
as that is the future my father meant.

A Pretty Wonderful Life

Flo and Vic on Ridge Road, 1975